Portuguese for Beginners

A Comprehensive Guide for Learning the
Portuguese Language Fast

Contents

AN INTRODUCTION

Are you...?

א   quite busy and in need of a precise, but thorough, resource to learn Portuguese?

א   traveling to or working in a Portuguese-speaking country?

Or do you...

א   want to connect with people, while keeping your personality[1] when speaking Portuguese, instead of just learning how to "tourist-talk"?

א   want to learn phrases that you can use to navigate social situations and help you make friends and new connections?

If your answer to these questions is "yes," then this book is here to help.

Let's start with a couple of questions: Is it worth learning a new language? And why Portuguese?

---

1 Fun fact: Studies show that personalities change when people are speaking a different language. If you're interested in this topic and want to know more, you can start by reading this: G. Marina Veltkamp, Guillermo Recio, Arthur M. Jacobs, and Markus Conrad. "Is personality modulated by language?" *International Journal of Bilingualism* 17, no. 4, 2013.

Well, it all comes down to a simple "*why not?*" This book could go on about all of the benefits it pays to your brain, in terms of your memory and other cognitive processes[2], but the learning of a new language undoubtedly transcends that very dispassionate, yet pragmatic, approach. Granted that if you are reading this, you have probably already decided to learn a new language, this guide will still take you through the thought process behind writing it and what you can expect from it.

Learning a new language is such an amazing tool that allows people from different parts of the world to connect more easily. That leads, more importantly, to deeper and more meaningful connections as well. In the case of the Portuguese language, several countries[3] have it as the official language, making it the sixth most spoken idiom on Earth, with 170 million speakers worldwide. This means that learning it grants you the possibility of making friends or finding job opportunities in the most obscure places you can imagine.[4]

---

2 The benefits of learning a new language have been known for years. For instance, we know that: bilinguals generally score higher on standardized math, reading, and vocabulary tests; have better focus, concentration, and attention; delay immediate gratification in the pursuit of long-term goals; have better memory and memorization skills, among many other positive effects. To check out a more detailed list, visit this page *https://www.sandiegounified.org/schools/sites/default/files_link/schools/files/Domain/18742/WORLD%20LANGUAGES%20Benefits%20of%20bilingualismarticle.pdf.* To further illustrate the idea, a small quote from an interesting article about how the learning of a language benefits cognition and mental processes: "(...) *new findings suggest that individuals benefit from that exposure, with greater openness to other languages and to new learning itself. At the other end of the lifespan, in old age, the active use of two or more languages appears to provide protection against cognitive decline.*" Kroll J., and Dussias P. *The Benefits of Multilingualism to the Personal and Professional Development of Residents of the US.*

3 Currently, ten countries have Portuguese as their official language: Brazil, Cape Verde, Angola, Guinea-Bissau, Equatorial-Guinea, São Tomé and Príncipe, Macau (technically, Macau isn't a country, but a special administrative region of China, alongside Hong Kong), East Timor, Mozambique, and, of course, Portugal.

4 There are even a lot of Portuguese speakers in other countries due to immigration or Portuguese influence: France, Switzerland, Luxembourg, Uruguay, Venezuela, and Guiana, just to name a few.

However, there is more to Portuguese than it just being a great tool of connection between fellow humans scattered around the world. Portuguese is immensely rich and full of music, history, and stories. It has come a long way, with the first form[5] of Portuguese dating back to the eighth century AD. This form was derived from the vulgar Latin spoken by the Romans, with influences from the Celts and other barbarian tribes that lived in the territory, which is now modern-day Portugal.[6]

And that is what this book wants to accomplish—to teach a language for all of the practical uses it holds while showcasing its essence, rhythm, and soul.

To do just that, aside from the fundamental chapters on how the language works, and for you to get in touch with the language and its applications in music, literature, and everyday events, the guide will occasionally have some notes about songs, poems, famous books, and idiomatic expressions that relate to what is being taught. Aside from the cultural richness and value that the content may possess by itself, reading literature or singing along to a Portuguese tune might just be the second-best way to learn a language and perfect the accent— besides trying to speak it with Portuguese speakers.

So, we finish as we started—Why learn Portuguese? What for? Is it worth it, or rather, *Vale a pena?*

The answer is very simple:

"Tudo vale a pena, se a alma não é pequena."[7]

---

5 Portuguese, as we know it now, is obviously very different from what the language was back then.

6 Fun fact: Portugal has had its defined borders since 1143 AD.

7 From the poem *Mar Português,* written by the famous Portuguese poet Fernando Pessoa. It means *"Is it worth it? Everything is worth it, if the soul isn't small."* For the full poem and an English adaptation, visit this blog:
http://literaryjoint.blogspot.com/2012/03/fernando-pessoa-mar-portugues.html.

Before we start, a heads-up

Anticipating the confusion that it may cause before we start; it is wise to remind you of the orthographic agreement this book follows.

Currently, only three countries adhere to the Portuguese Orthographic Agreement of 1991. This international treaty was created to unite the language in the countries where Portuguese is the official idiom. It changed various aspects of the language (for instance, the rules of capitalization), but nothing so fundamental that it could preclude somebody that learned the language using one system, not to understand it in the other system.

Despite this—and admitting beforehand that it is also my stand on the issue—many Portuguese writers do not approve of the agreement, and thus don't write accordingly. In contrast, some countries didn't even adhere to it, regardless of having ratified it.[8]

It really won't make that much of a difference to you. Still, keep that information in mind just so that if you happen to see some words

---

8 Despite the ratification of the treaty in 1991, Portugal only signed the agreement into law in 2008. It was then officially implemented by the government after a six-year transition process.

spelled slightly differently,[9] you know why. However, just in case, always double-check. In a best-case scenario, you will spot a mistake that somebody (just like myself), who is probably a native, made. Let's say, for instance, that you are exchanging messages with a Portuguese friend and he/she says:

"Foi um acto cruel!" ↶ "It was a cruel act!"

You should say, "Em vez de 'ACTO,' não se escreve '*ATO*' agora?" ↶ Instead of "'ACT,' isn't it written 'ACT' now?"

And well, isn't that something to brag about?

---

9 This can happen if you read Portuguese from a country that is not Portugal since it may vary slightly from place to place. For instance, at the end of this book, you will find a list of words that are written differently in the Portuguese from Brazil. I want to stress that both forms are orthographically correct.

PART I: THE VERY BASICS

The Portuguese Alphabet[10]

Like the English alphabet, the Portuguese alphabet is based on the Latin or Roman alphabet and consists of 26 letters. Nevertheless, the pronunciation of each letter might be different than the way it is pronounced in English. Plus, many sounds are unique to the language or at least are not very common in English. So, let's start by learning how to pronounce each letter. It is not as simple as it may appear—depending on where the letter is in a word, its pronunciation will be quite different. Ok, maybe it isn't *that* different, but it might be different enough to sound weird if not said the correct way. Furthermore, you most likely want to be understood and impress people when you are speaking Portuguese. Thus, you want to get it just right!

Vowels

Let's start with the vowels[11]: A, E, I, O, U. That is easy, but how are they pronounced?

---

10 If you want to sing the alphabet in European Portuguese, check out this video: https://www.youtube.com/watch?v=aBNGZjjxOS0.

11 Looking for a fun way to practice the pronunciation of the vowels? Check out this song: https://www.youtube.com/watch?v=0ZXcE2YKV34.

א   "**A**" – like the "A" in "BAR"

א   "**E**" – like the "A" in "WELL"

א   "**I**" – like the "EE" in "FEED"

א   "**O**" – like the "O" in "MORE"

א   "**U**" – like the "O" in "LOSE"

However, as mentioned, the pronunciation might change: If the letters are surrounded by other letters, if they are at the beginning, middle, or end of a word, if they have a diacritical mark, and so on. There are four big types of pronunciation. Let's see how each letter's sound changes depending on what pronunciation type we are talking about.

א   **Open pronunciation**[12]:

A) The open pronunciation of the letter "A" in Portuguese sounds like the "A" in "FAR." It is the correct pronunciation most of the times when "A" is the stressed syllable of the word, like the first "A" in the word "CALMA - CALM," or if it contains the diacritical mark (acute accent) " ´ " like in the word "ALIÁS - BESIDES, INDEED."

E) The open pronunciation of the letter "E" in Portuguese sounds like the "E" in "VET." It is the correct pronunciation most of the times when "E" is the stressed syllable of the word, like the one in "SERRA[13] - MOUNTAIN RANGE," or if it contains the diacritical mark (acute accent) " ´ " like in the word "PÉ - FOOT."

I) The letter "I" is almost always pronounced with an open sound, like the "EE" in "FLEE": "FICAR - STAY; SORRIR - SMILE; GRITAR - SCREAM."

O) The open pronunciation of the letter "O" sounds like the "O" in "CORE." It is the correct pronunciation most of the times

---

12 A good way to memorize is to remember that in open pronunciation, you have to have your mouth wide open to pronounce it.

13 "Serra" can also mean "saw."

when the "O" is the stressed syllable of the word, like in the word "SOL - SUN," or if it contains the diacritical mark (acute accent) " ´ ", like in the word "SÓ - ALONE."

U) "U" is almost always pronounced with an open sound, like the "OO" in the word "COOPER": "UM - ONE; LUZ - LIGHT; LUA - MOON."

As you may have noticed, the open pronunciation is the one we use when saying (or singing if we want it to be more fun) the vowels by themselves: **a, e, i, o, u**. Now, what about the other types of pronunciation? You also probably observed that within the same word, the vowels have different sounds. Let's keep going.

ℵ Closed pronunciation[14]:

A) The closed pronunciation of the letter "A" sounds like the "A" in the word "MAYBE." It happens when the "A" is at the end of a word, but not exclusively. Remember the word "CALMA - CALM"? The second "A" has the closed pronunciation.

E) The closed pronunciation of the letter "E" sounds like the "E" in "CLOSED." It happens when the "E" is *not* at the end of the word, but it can be in the stressed syllable. For instance: "PECAR - ([TO] SIN)."

O) The closed pronunciation of the letter "O" sounds like the "O" in "SOAP." It happens when the "O" is *not* at the end of the word, but it can be in the stressed syllable, just like the first "O" in the word "OVO - EGG." It is very similar to the nasal pronunciation.

ℵ Reduced pronunciation[15]:

E) The reduced pronunciation occurs when the "E" is at the end of the word, like in "VONTADE - WILL."

---

14 Here, the trick is to close your lips when saying the letter.

15 When using the reduced pronunciation, it is almost like you are stopping yourself before finishing the word.

A, I, O, U) There are not, from my point of view, good examples for these other letters. The differences are so small and so irrelevant that trying to explain them would be needless and perhaps more confusing.

ℵ **Nasal pronunciation**[16]:

A) The nasal pronunciation happens when the "A" precedes an "M" or an "N" like in "ANTES - BEFORE," or when it has the diacritical marks "^" or "~" like in the word "MAÇÃ - APPLE." It sounds similar to the "U" in the word "HUNG."

E) The nasal pronunciation happens when the "E" precedes an "M" or "N" like in the word "GENTE - PEOPLE," or when it has the diacritical marks "^" or "~" like in the word "PÊRA - PEAR." It sounds like the first "E" in the word "EMBARRASSED."

O) The nasal pronunciation happens when the "O" is followed by an "M" or "N" like in the word "ONTEM - YESTERDAY," or the when it has the diacritical marks "^" or "~" like in the word "CÔCO - COCONUT." It sounds similar to the "O" in the word "OVER." Again, it is very similar to the closed pronunciation.

Then, whenever we have two vowels together that we read in one go, instead of pronouncing very clearly each letter, we are talking about diphthongs. It is like the sound of each vowel individually blends with the other, making it one sound, instead of the separate sound of each vowel. So, in Portuguese, we have oral and nasal diphthongs. The oral diphthongs are: "**ai, au, ei, oi, ou, ui.**" The nasal diphthongs are: "**ão, õe, ãos, ões, ães.**" They will be especially easy to pronounce when you have a cold!

---

16 The trick here is pretty easy—just block, close, cover, your nostrils with your fingers to make that funny nasal sound.

Now, let's take a look at the rest of the letters. They are, as you already know, B, C, D, F, G, H, J, K, L, M, N, P, Q, R, S, T, V, W, X, Y, Z. Although most do not differ much from what the English pronunciation is, there are many variations and a lot of sounds that a single letter can make, depending on which letters surround it. Just like with the vowels, let's take a look at each one.

א   **B (bê)** - The "B" in a word sounds just like the one in the English "bola ↝ ball."

א   **C (cê)** - The "C" has a lot of different sounds. It may have a soft sound, just like the "C" in "CITY." That happens when the next letter is either an "E" or "I," like in the word "CERA ↝ WAX." When the "C" is followed by an "A," "O," "U," or a consonant, it has a hard sound as in the "C" in "COURT." Like, for instance, in the word "CARRO ↝ CAR" or "CRER ↝ (TO) BELIEVE." Then, we have an exception. The pair "CH" does not make the "C" have a hard sound, nor the sound that the "CH" pair makes in English. Instead, it has the same sound as the "SH" pair in English, just like in the word "SHE." As an example: "CHUVA ↝ RAIN." Finally, we have the "Ç." We call it "C Cedilhado" or "C com cedilha." The cedilla is used to turn a hard sound into a soft one. So, let's take, for instance, "CAÇAR ↝ HUNT." If the "C" did not have the cedilla, it would make a hard sound instead of the soft one it is supposed to make.

א   **D (dê)** - It has the same sound as the "D" in the word "DOLL."

א   **F (éfe)** - It has the same sound as the "F" in the word "FUDGE."

---

17 Between parenthesis, you will find the way to pronounce each consonant by itself. Remember what you have learned from the pronunciation of the vowels, or go back if you need to.

℘ **G (gê)** – The "G" might have two different sounds—a hard or soft one. The hard sound happens when it is followed by an "A," "O," or "U," just like the "G" in the word "GANG." Example: "GUARDA ↝ GUARD." When followed by an "E" or "I," it sounds just like a "J."

℘ **H (hagá)** – The "H" is always silent in Portuguese. However, as we already know, when paired with a "C" (always in this order "CH"), it changes the sound of the "C."

℘ **J (jota)** – Regardless of what vowel is after, "J" is always pronounced like the "S" in "MEASURE," no matter what vowel follows it. Example: "JOGO ↝ GAME." Fun fact: In Spain, it is pronounced like a hard "R," which we will see in a bit.

℘ **K (kápa)** – The "K" is pronounced the same way in both languages. And the "Q" in the same way "K" is.

℘ **L (éle)** – The "L" has the same pronunciation in the English language, but that depends on whether we encounter it at the beginning of a word, like in "LATE," and between vowels, like in "ELASTIC," or at the end of a word, like in "SHOVEL." However, there is one exception that we do not see—or rather hear—in English. When an "H" follows the "L," the sound it makes is somewhat strange. You can achieve it by touching the ceiling of your mouth with your tongue and pushing it against your teeth while trying to say something like "LHE."[18]

℘ **M (éme)** – "M" has the same sound it has in English (like the "M" in "MALL") if we see it at the beginning of a word, like in the word "MALUCO ↝ CRAZY" or between vowels, like in the word "AMAR ↝ (TO) LOVE." However, it can have a different sound, just like the "N" in "ANT." That happens when we encounter it at the end of a word, like in "(ELES) FICAM ↝ (THEY'LL) STAY."

---

18 I know it is quite hard to explain via writing. To hear it and grab a better understanding of what it's supposed to sound like with some examples, check out this video, which is in English: https://www.youtube.com/watch?v=ElMCAOwBHns.

א **N (éne)** - It has the same hard sound as the "N" in the word "NEVER" if it is at the beginning of a word or between vowels; but if we find it between a vowel and a consonant, it has the same soft sound as in English, just like the "N" in the word "PANTS." However, when an "H" comes after it, it makes a similar sound to the "LH" sound, but with an "N" instead of an "L" sound.[19]

א **P (pê)** - It has the same sound as the "P" in the word "PARK."

א **Q (qê)** - It has the same sound as the "K" in the word "PARK." However, we have to pay attention to a few details. It is always followed by the letter "U"; however, the letter "U" is not always read. Whenever an "E" or "I" comes after the "QU," the "U" is silent, like in "(EU) QUERO ↶ (I)WANT" or "QUILÓMETRO ↶ KILOMETRE." If it is an "A" or "O" that follows, the "U" is read aloud, just like in "QUALQUER ↶ ANY/WHICHEVER" and "QUOCIENTE ↶ QUOTIENT."

א **R (érre)** - This letter has a similar sound to the English "R" when we find it at the end of a word, or before or after a vowel, just like in the word "MARCA ↶ BRAND" or "ADICIONAR ↶ (TO) ADD." But it can also have a hard sound, and that is when it is either a double "RR," or when we find it at the beginning of a word. To make it, try imitating the purr of a cat!

א **S (ésse)** - This letter has many different pronunciations. It has the same sound that we know from English when we encounter it at the beginning of a word, or when it is a doubled "SS," just like in the words "SOL↶ SUN" and "ASSADO ↶ ROASTED." However, before a consonant, it makes the sound we already know from the "SH" pair, like in the word "COSTA ↶

---

19 Ok, if you still need more help, check out this video and hear how to say it: https://www.youtube.com/watch?v=DCRuTNDPdKw.

COAST." Finally, between two vowels, it sounds like a "Z," like in the word "USAR ↝ (TO) USE."

ℵ   **T (tê)** - It has the same sound as the "T" in the word "TOY."

ℵ   **V (vê)** - It has the same sound as the "V" in the word "VASE."

ℵ   **X (xiz)** – This letter also has many different pronunciations—a total of five! The problem with this letter is that it has no rule, so you will always have to check how to say it correctly. To start, the most common sound is the "CH" sound, which we already know, like in "XADREZ ↝ CHESS" (the equivalent to the "SH" in English). It also may sound like a "hard C" and "S" together, just like the "X" in the word "BOX." It can have the "Z" sound, like in the word "EXAME ↝ EXAM." Finally, it can make the "SS" sound, like in the word "MÁXIMO ↝ MAXIMUM."

ℵ   **Y (ípsilon)** - It has the same sound as the letter "I." It is only used in neologisms and foreign words.

ℵ   **W (dabliú)** – Since it is also only used in neologisms and foreign words, it either can sound like a "U" or "V."

ℵ   **Z (zê)** – It has the same sound as the "Z" in the word "ZOMBIE." However, when we find it at the end of a word, it sounds like "SH" as in "SHE." Example: "GIZ ↝ CHALK."

But with all this knowledge, how do we know how to read complete words? Which syllable is the stressed one?

You already know that if a vowel has an accent, whichever one it is, that is the syllable you accentuate. However, if there is no diacritical mark, what is the rule? Then, and usually, the stress of the word goes into the penultimate syllable. Take, for instance, the word "CO-**RA**-GEM ↝ COURAGE"—the stress is in the middle, in the syllable "RA."

There are a few exceptions, though. Let's go through them. Words ending in "I," "IM," "INS," "L," "R," "UM," "UNS,"and "Z" have their stress shift to the last syllable. Read out loud the next examples, and do not forget to shift the stress to the last syllable of the word.

- ℵ   RE-QUE-*RI* ↶ (I) REQUIRED
- ℵ   MU-SI-*CAL* ↶ MUSICAL
- ℵ   MA-NE-*QUIM* ↶ MANNEQUIN
- ℵ   MA-NE-*QUINS* ↶ MANNEQUINS
- ℵ   CIN-TI-*LAR* ↶ SPARKLE
- ℵ   IN-CO-*MUM* ↶ UNCOMMON
- ℵ   IN-CO-*MUNS* ↶ UNCOMMON (pl.)
- ℵ   ES-TU-PI-*DEZ* ↶ STUPIDITY

Numbers, Days of the Week, Months, Seasons, and Telling the Time

Numbers

Did you know that the Portuguese use the Arabic numerals? Did you know that Americans and the vast majority of countries use them, too?[20] Well, what did you expect—that we would still use the Roman numerals? How do you say those in Portuguese, though? Let's see:

- ℵ   0 - Zero
- ℵ   1 - Um
- ℵ   2 - Dois
- ℵ   3 - Três
- ℵ   4 - Quatro
- ℵ   5 - Cinco
- ℵ   6 - Seis
- ℵ   7 - Sete

---

20 The answer to the question, apparently, is not that obvious:
https://www.independent.co.uk/news/arabic-numerals-survey-prejudice-bias-survey-research-civic-science-a8918256.html.

- א 8 - Oito
- א 9 - Nove
- א 10 - Dez
- א 11 - Onze
- א 12 - Doze
- א 13 - Treze
- א 14 - Catorze
- א 15 - Quinze
- א 16 - Dezasseis
- א 17 - Dezassete
- א 18 - Dezoito
- א 19 - Dezanove
- א 20 - Vinte
- א 30 - Trinta
- א 40 - Quarenta
- א 50 - Cinquenta
- א 60 - Sessenta
- א 70 - Setenta
- א 80 - Oitenta
- א 90 - Noventa
- א 100 - Cem
- א 200 - Duzentos
- א 300 - Trezentos
- א 400 - Quatrocentos
- א 500 - Quinhentos
- א 600 - Seiscentos
- א 700 - Setecentos
- א 800 - Oitocentos
- א 900 - Novecentos
- א 1000 - Mil
- א 1.000.000 - Um milhão

Now, you have all that you need to "create" the numbers between the ones indicated above. So, between 20 and 30, you just do what you would in English—add the number in front of the set of the ten. Like so:

ℵ   21 – Twenty-one ↶ Vinte e um

ℵ   22 – Twenty-two ↶ Vinte e dois

ℵ   23 – Twenty-three ↶ Vinte e três

ℵ   207 – Two-hundred and seven ↶ Duzentos e sete

ℵ   310 – Three-hundred and ten ↶ Trezentos e dez

ℵ   450 – Four hundred and fifty ↶ Quatrocentos e cinquenta

ℵ   573 – Five hundred and seventy-three ↶ Quinhentos e setenta e três

ℵ   1100 – One thousand one hundred ↶ Mil e cem

ℵ   83.100 – Eighty-three thousand one hundred ↶ Oitenta e três mil e cem

You get the point. There is an exception, though. When it comes to "a hundred ↶ cem," when saying the numbers that come after, let's say, for instance, "101," you don't say "cem e um." Instead, it works like this:

ℵ   101 – One hundred and one ↶ **Cento** e um

ℵ   70.102 – Seventy thousand, one hundred and two ↶ Setenta mil, **cento** e dois

ℵ   1.839.154 – One million, eight hundred and thirty-nine thousand, one hundred and fifty-four ↶ Um milhão, oitocentos e trinta e nove mil, **cento** e cinquenta e quatro

From this point on, everything is the same. Still, it is worth paying attention to what a billion is in English because, in Portuguese, the similar word a "bilião" depicts a different reality:

ℵ   1.000.000.000 – Mil milhões ↶ Billion

ℵ   1.000.000.000.000 – Um bilião ↶ Trillion

ℵ   1.000.000.000.000.000 – Mil trilião ↶ Quadrillion

As for the ordinal numbers, let's see the first ten.

ℵ   First ↝ Primeiro

ℵ   Second ↝ Segundo

ℵ   Third ↝ Terceiro

ℵ   Forth ↝ Quarto

ℵ   Fifth ↝ Quinto

ℵ   Sixth ↝ Sexto

ℵ   Seventh ↝ Sétimo

ℵ   Eight ↝ Oitavo

ℵ   Nineth ↝ Nono

ℵ   Tenth ↝ Décimo

ℵ   Twentieth ↝ Vigésimo

ℵ   Thirtieth ↝Trigésimo

ℵ   Fortieth ↝ Quadragésimo

ℵ   Fiftieth ↝ Quinquagésimo

ℵ   Sixtieth ↝ Sexagésimo

ℵ   Seventieth ↝ Septagésimo

ℵ   Eightieth ↝ Octogésimo

ℵ   Ninetieth ↝ Nonagésimo

ℵ   Hundreth ↝ Centésimo

You need to add the ordinal number, needed from the first ten we saw, between each set of ten. However, notice that both numbers are in their ordinal form and not just the second. Like so:

ℵ   Twenty-first ↝ Vigésimo primeiro

ℵ   Thirty-second ↝ Trigésimo segundo

ℵ   Fifty-fifth ↝ Quinquagésimo quinto

And so on...

Days of the Week

The Portuguese names for the days of the week have an old and interesting origin. Every workday has the suffix "feira," and supposedly, the first day of the week is called "**segunda**-feira," which means "second"—as you know. Why is this?

Most of the idioms around the world have the names of the week's days based on the visible planets from Earth—Mercury, Venus, Mars, Jupiter, Saturn—plus the moon and the sun, while a few others are based on mythological figures[21]. So, in the original Latin, born in the Late Antiquity period and from there on out, the days of the week were called:

- א   *Dies solis* - Day of the sun
- א   *Dies lunae* - Day of the moon
- א   *Dies martis* - Day of Mars
- א   *Dies mercurii* - Day of Mercury
- א   *Dies iovis* - Day of Jupiter
- א   *Dies veneris* - Day of Venus
- א   *Dies saturni* - Day of Saturn

The Portuguese language is the only one in the romance languages' family that does not follow the rule. This is because São Martinho de Dume, a Portuguese bishop, thought it would be a blasphemy to give pagan names to the week's days during the Holy Week. This happened around 563 BC. He then proposed that during the Holy Week (in the Middle Ages this was solely dedicated to rest and prayers), the Christians should refer to Sunday as the Day of the Lord, and to the following days, as "free" days, days of rest, in numerical order. So:

- א   *Dominicus* ↪ *Dies Domini* ↪ Domingo
- א   *Feria secunda* ↪ *Secunda feria* ↪ Segunda-feira
- א   *Feria tertia* ↪ *Tertia feria* ↪ Terça-feira
- א   *Feria quarta* ↪ *Quarta feria* ↪ Quarta-feira

---

21 For instance, the English "Thursday" has its origin in the Old English, in Thor's Day, the God of Thunder.

אַ   *Feria quinta* ↝ *Quinta feria* ↝ Quinta-feira

אַ   *Feria sexta* ↝ *Sexta feria* ↝ Sexta-feira

אַ   *Sabbath[22]* ↝ *Sabatum* ↝ Sábado

Needless to say, the proposal lasted way beyond its original idea of being applied during the Holy Week.

So, initially, the word "feria" meant literally "rest" or "free day." The word evolved to "feira," which means "fair"[23] in English, but now you know its true origin. Additionally, the Portuguese word for "vacation" today is very similar to what it was back then—"férias."

Was it a boring story? As boring and difficult as getting through a typical Monday? Well, it is only appropriate that we get to work then...

אַ   Days of the week ↝ Dias da semana

אַ   Workdays/business days ↝ Dias úteis

אַ   Monday ↝ Segunda-feira

אַ   Tuesday ↝ Terça-feira

אַ   Wednesday ↝ Quarta-feira

אַ   Thursday ↝ Quinta-feira

אַ   Friday ↝ Sexta-feira[24]

אַ   Saturday ↝ Sábado

אַ   Sunday ↝ Domingo

אַ   Weekend ↝ Fim-de-semana

אַ   Day ↝ Dia

אַ   Week ↝ Semana

אַ   Weekly ↝ Semanal

---

[22] As you may know, the "SABBATH" is the Jewish day destined for rest, which occurred at the end of the week. So, traditionally, that was when the week ended.

23 As in "medieval fair" and not as in "just," which would be "justo" or "correcto."

24 If you want to hear a song in which you can practice your pronunciation of "Sexta-feira," check out this Portuguese band: https://www.youtube.com/watch?v=6gIQx5P9Xl0.

א   Tomorrow ᔕ Amanhã

א   The day after tomorrow ᔕ Depois de amanhã

א   Yesterday ᔕ Ontem

א   The day before yesterday ᔕ Anteontem

א   Day off ᔕ Folga

Months

Now, let's take a look at the months of the year. When it comes to the names of the months in Portuguese, there is another story to tell. Did you know that there were only ten months originally in Ancient Rome? That is due to the creator of Rome, Romulus, who gave the name to the old city.

So, we had "MARCH," which was dedicated to *Martius*, the god of war. Then came "APRIL." Some say it was dedicated to *Aphrodite*, the goddess of love, while others defend that it derives from the word "APERIRE - ABRIR ᔕ TO OPEN," related to the opening of the flowers during that time in the Northern Hemisphere. Then "MAY," which was named after the goddess *Maia,* responsible for the growth of plants and flowers. Then "JUNE" or *Juno,* goddess of wedding and birth. Then "JULY," which was initially called "*Quintiles*" since it was the fifth month of the year. However, it was later rebaptized to pay homage to Julius Caesar. "AUGUST" was also rebaptized to celebrate the emperor, Caesar Augustus. Before that, it was named "*Sextilis.*" Finally, "SEPTEMBER," "OCTOBER," "NOVEMBER," and "DECEMBER" were all named after the Latin words that mean, respectively, seventh, eighth, ninth, and tenth.

However, when the successor of Romulus, Pompilius, rose to power, he added two more months to coincide the twelve months with a lunar cycle.

So, "JANUARY" was added as the first year. It was a homage to *Jano,* a god of two faces, also considered the god of beginnings, and that is why it was named as the first month of the year. Then came

"FEBRUARY," which was a reference to the god of purification, called *Februa*. That is why this month has fewer days than the others!

Now, let's dive straight into our list.

- ℵ   Months ↝ Meses
- ℵ   January ↝ Janeiro
- ℵ   February ↝ Fevereiro
- ℵ   March ↝ Março
- ℵ   April ↝ Abril
- ℵ   May ↝ Maio
- ℵ   June ↝ Junho
- ℵ   July ↝ Julho
- ℵ   August ↝ Agosto
- ℵ   September ↝ Setembro
- ℵ   October ↝ Outubro
- ℵ   November ↝ Novembro
- ℵ   December ↝ Dezembro
- ℵ   Monthly ↝ Mensalmente
- ℵ   Trimester ↝ Trimestre
- ℵ   Semester ↝ Semestre

Seasons

Now, let's take a look at the "épocas do ano!"

- ℵ   Annual ↝ Anual
- ℵ   Leap year ↝ Ano bissexto
- ℵ   Spring ↝ Primavera
- ℵ   Summer ↝ Verão
- ℵ   Autumn/Fall ↝ Outono
- ℵ   Winter ↝ Inverno
- ℵ   Easter ↝ Páscoa
- ℵ   Christmas ↝ Natal
- ℵ   Christmas Eve ↝ Véspera de Natal/Consoada

א   New Year ↶ Ano Novo

א   New Year's Eve↶ Véspera de Ano Novo

א   April Fool's Day ↶ Dia das Mentiras

א   Halloween ↶ Dia das Bruxas

א   Vacations ↶ Férias

א   Holidays ↶ Feriados

א   Valentine's Day ↶ Dia dos Namorados

Telling the Time

Now you know the Portuguese letters, vowels, consonants, numbers, days of the week, months, and seasons, it is time to learn about just that—time!

Portugal's time zone is WET (Western Europe Time), which can be represented by UTC+0. During summer, it is the WEST (Western Europe Summertime) or DST, or UTC+1. Unlike in the United States, for instance, the official format used in Portugal is the 24-hour format. So, every hour after 12 p.m. would just go on in numerical order until the 24th hour (which corresponds to the hour 0), instead of just going back to 1 p.m. This way, the official way to say the time if it is 5.30 p.m., would be 17h30; 12 p.m. - 12h; 1 p.m. - 13h; 2 p.m. - 14h; 3 p.m. - 15h; 4 p.m. - 16h; 5 p.m. - 17h; and so on.

Despite this, you will definitely hear or read something like: «I'll meet you "às *3 da tarde.*"» or «I'll be there "*às 11 da manhã.*"» or "The concert is "*às 9 da noite.*"» This is because, in informal conversations, it is more common to use **"de manhã"** to indicate a time during the morning—a.m.—and **"da tarde"** and **"da noite"** to indicate the time during the afternoon and night—p.m.

Classes of Words

Did you know there are a total of ten classes of words in the Portuguese language? That's right: the determiners, the pronouns, the nouns, the adjectives, the verbs, the conjunctions, the prepositions, the adverbs, the numerals, and the interjections. You probably studied them in school around the fourth grade. In Portuguese, there are a lot of things that might be different but do not worry—many other things you will surely recognize or be familiar with. Besides, what is not familiar won't be very hard.

Take a look at a few examples of each class of words:

The numerals you have already studied. They correspond to the numbers mentioned in the previous chapter—they evidently indicate quantity or a place in a specific order. In the next chapter, we will look at the verbs and how to conjugate them in three different tenses. The following sections will focus on the study of the nouns, determiners, pronouns, prepositions, adjectives, and adverbs.

Nouns

Let's start with the nouns, also known as substantives. In Portuguese, you can also say "substantivo ∽ substantive," but the translation for "nouns" is "nomes ∽ names." Nouns are words that designate people, things, animals, actions, qualities, or states.

Determiners	Nouns	Adjectives	Verbs	Numerals
O	Crianças	Loura	Estar	Um
(a) Minha	Rapaz	Engraçado	Brincar	Dois
Um	Aluno	Inteligente	Faltar	Dez
Este	Escola	Grande	Ir	Primeiro
Aquele	Lisboa	Esforçada	Sentir	Quinto

There five sub-classes of nouns

ℵ   Proper nouns

ℵ   Common nouns

ℵ   Abstract nouns

ℵ   Concrete nouns

ℵ   Collective nouns

The proper nouns indicate individualized beings—people, things, or animals—and are usually written with an uppercase. Common nouns also indicate beings—people, things, or animals—but these are not individualized and are usually written with a lowercase. The same

Pronouns	Prepositions	Conjunctions	Adverbs	Interjections
Ele	Até	Quando	Aqui	Ena!
Ela	Com	Enquanto	Ali	Ui!
Lhe	De	Mas	Longe	Ai!
Se	Em	E	Tarde	Socorro!
Meu	Por	Pois	Docemente	Ah!

word can be a proper noun and a common noun; it depends on the sentence and context. Take a look at these sentences to see just that:

ℵ   "A **Rosa Coelho** foi à **Figueira da Foz**. ↶ Rosa Coelho[25] went to Figueira da Foz[26]."

ℵ   "Esta **rosa** é linda. ↶ This rose is beautiful."

ℵ   "Ontem comi **coelho** ao jantar. ↶ Yesterday I had rabbit for dinner."

ℵ   "Aquela **figueira** está cheia de figos. ↶ That fig tree is full of figs."

ℵ   "Ali fica a **foz** do rio Sado. ↶ Over there is the river Sado's mouth."

In the first sentence, all of the nouns highlighted are proper nouns. The first two, "Rosa" and "Coelho," are names, and the third is the name of a city. The second sentence used "coelho" as well, but this time as a common noun. The third sentence has part of the name of the city we saw in the first sentence—"figueira"—again used as a common noun. Finally, in the fourth sentence, we have the other word that composes the name of the city, "foz"; this time also used as a common noun.

Then, as a sub-subclass of the common nouns, we have the abstract nouns. They indicate actions, qualities, or states. The other sub-subclass of the common nouns are the concrete nouns. They indicate people, things, or animals.

ℵ   "Uma **amiga** minha está no **hospital** com o seu **cão**. ↶ A friend of mine is at the hospital with her dog."

ℵ   "Os médicos têm **esperança** na sua **recuperação**. ↶ The doctors have hope in her recovery."

In the first sentence, we are facing three concrete nouns; in the second sentence, two abstract nouns—"esperança" and "recuperação."

---

25 "Coelho" means rabbit, but it is also a last name in Portuguese.

26 "Figueira da Foz" is a city in the central region of Portugal, near Coimbra.

The word "médicos" in the second sentence is a collective noun, which we will talk about next.

Finally, we have the collective nouns that indicate a group of various elements of the same species or type. For instance:

ℵ   "Uma **multidão** observa o incêndio que consome o **arvoredo**, já perto do **casario**[27]. ↶ A crowd observes the fire that consumes the grove, already near to the houses."

Determiners

Determiners are words that, variating in gender or number, precede the noun, giving us information about it. Basically, we know more details about what we are talking about because of the determiners. They can specify—determine—what we are talking about. For instance, a determiner will indicate:

ℵ   If we are talking about a man or woman

ℵ   If there is one object or many in a given area

ℵ   In which position an object is in space

ℵ   To whom an object belongs to

Hence, there are several sub-classes of determiners:

ℵ   Definite articles

ℵ   Indefinite articles

ℵ   Demonstrative determiners

ℵ   Possessive determiners

ℵ   Interrogative determiners

ℵ   Indefinite determiners

ℵ   Numeral Determiners

Bear in mind that, in English, the determiners "the," "a," and "an" correspond to all of the articles we are going study—the reason being,

---

27 "Casario" is an agglomeration of houses.

as mentioned, that the determiners in Portuguese vary in gender and number.

Let's start at the beginning—the **definite articles**:

Singular		Plural	
Masculine	Feminine	Masculine	Feminine
O	A	Os	As

The definite articles indicate objects, things, or people that are specified and perfectly well known. It implies that something is a specific thing or many specific things. Like so:

א   "<u>O</u> livro. ↪ The book."

א   "<u>A</u> sala de estar. ↪ The living room."

א   "<u>Os</u> gatos. ↪ The cats."

א   "<u>As</u> mãos. ↪ The hands."

As for the **indefinite articles**:

Singular		Plural	
Masculine	Feminine	Masculine	Feminine
Um	Uma	Uns	Umas

The indefinite articles designate objects or people that are not perfectly well known. Basically, they aren't specified. Let's see a few sentences in which they are used:

א   "É <u>um</u> quadro lindo! ↪ It is a beautiful painting."

א   "Eu quero comer <u>uma</u> maçã. ↪ I want to eat an apple."

א   "<u>Uns</u> rapazes passaram por aqui. ↪ A few guys passed by."

א   "Tu deste-me <u>umas</u> camisas. ↪ You gave me some shirts."

As for the **demonstrative determiners**:

Singular		Plural	
Masculine	**Feminine**	**Masculine**	**Feminine**
Este (This)	Esta	Estes (These)	Estas
Esse (That)	Essa	Esses (Those)	Essas
Aquele (That, but further away than "esse")	Aquela	Aqueles (Those, but further away than "esses"	Aquelas
O outro (The other)	A outra	Os outros	As outras
O mesmo (The same)	A mesma	Os mesmos	As mesmas
Tal		Tais	
Isto (this or this thing right here)			
Isso (That or that thing—further away than "this," but closer than "aquilo"			
Aquilo (That thing over there)			

The demonstrative determiners indicate the position of an object in place or time. They help a lot in knowing where exactly something is regarding those other things around it. Ok, maybe not exactly, but it will definitely point you in the right direction. For instance:

א   "**Esta** comida é óptima. ↵ This food is great."

א   "Dá-me **esse** livro. ↵ Give me that book."

א   "Não é esse, é **aquele** livro ao fundo da prateleira. ↵ It isn't *that* one, it's that one by the end of the shelf."

As for the **possessive determiners:**

Singular		Plural	
Masculine	**Feminine**	**Masculine**	**Feminine**
Meu (Mine)	Minha	Meus	Minhas
Teu (Yours)	Tua	Teus	Tuas
Seu (His)	Sua (Hers)	Seus	Suas
Nosso (Ours)	Nossa	Nossos	Nossas
Vosso (Yours)	Vossa	Vossos	Vossas
Seu (Theirs)[28]	Sua	Seus	Suas

The possessive determiners express an idea of possession. So, to say that something is yours, or someone else's, you would use the possessive determiners indicated above. Like so:

ℵ   "Aquela é a **minha** casa. ↪ That is my house."

ℵ   "A **tua** caneta. ↪ Your pen."

ℵ   "O vinho é **nosso**! ↪ The wine is ours!"

ℵ   "As cadeiras não são **vossas**. ↪ The chairs are not yours."

---

[28] Instead of "SEU," you will hear natives saying "DELES." It is the word that's used most often—by far!

As for the **interrogative determiners**:

Singular		Plural	
Masculine	**Feminine**	**Masculine**	**Feminine**
Quanto (How much)	Quanta	Quantos (How many)	Quantas
Qual (Which one)		Quais (Which ones)	
Quem (Who, whom)			
Que (What)			

These determiners exist to introduce interrogations, to ask questions. So, for instance:

ℵ   "**Quanto** custa uma garrafa de sumo? ↪ How much is a bottle of wine?"

ℵ   "**Qual** é o teu nome? ↪ What is your name?"

ℵ   "**Quem** és? ↪ Who are you?"

ℵ   "**Que** fazes aqui? ↪ What are you doing here?"

As for the **indefinite determiners**:

Singular		Plural	
Masculine	**Feminine**	**Masculine**	**Feminine**
Algum (Any, something)	Alguma	Alguns (Some)	Algumas
Nenhum (None)	Nenhuma	Nenhuns	Nenhumas
Todo (All)	Toda	Todos	Todas

Certo[29] (Certain)	Certa	Certos	Certas
Muito (A lot, many, quite)	Muita	Muitos (Many)	Muitas
Outro (Other)	Outra	Outros (Others)	Outras
Pouco (Little, not much)	Pouca	Poucos (Few)	Poucas
Tanto (Much, such)	Tanta	Tantos (Many)	Tantas
Qualquer (Any)		Quaisquer	
Tudo (Everything)			
Nada (Nothing)			
Cada (Each)			
Alguém (Someone, somebody)			
Ninguém (No one, nobody)			

The indefinite determiners indicate beings or things in an imprecise way, not specified. Take the following examples to make things clearer:

 ℵ "Alguém está aqui. ↵ Somebody is here."

 ℵ "Ninguém está aqui. ↵ Nobody is here."

 ℵ "Nenhum homem come tanto como eu! ↵ No man eats as much as I do."

---

[29] It can also mean "CORRECT" or "RIGHT."

א   "Qualquer coisa serve! ↵ Anything is fine."

You can see that—very similar to what the indefinite articles do concerning nouns—the indefinite determiners cast a general idea, an imprecise not specified detail about the situation or what is going to happen.

Finally, as for the **numeral determiners**, they correspond to the numbers you studied in the previous chapter.

Pronouns

We already talked about nouns and determiners, so now it is time to deal with the pronouns. Pronouns substitute the nouns—they exist in a sentence to represent a noun. There are six types of pronouns:

א   Personal pronouns

א   Demonstrative pronouns

א   Possessive pronouns

א   Relative pronouns

א   Interrogative pronouns

א   Indefinite pronouns

In this chapter, we are going to focus on the personal, demonstrative, and possessive pronouns and how to use them in a sentence. Let's dive right in.

א   Personal pronouns

These are the most important, and more frequently used, in speech and writing:

א   "EU" ↵ in English it would translate to "I"

א   "TU" ↵ in English it would translate to "YOU"

א   "ELE" ↵ in English it would translate to "HE"

א   "ELA" ↵ in English it would translate to "SHE"

א   "NÓS" ↵ in English it would translate to "US"

א   "VÓS" ↵ in English it would translate to "WE"

א   "ELES" ↶ applied to a group of feminine subjects, in English it would translate to "THEY"

א   "ELAS" ↶ applied to a group of masculine subjects, in English it would translate to "THEY"

These sets of pronouns directly designate the subject of a sentence. They work just like the pronouns work in the English language—you just have to substitute the noun for the corresponding pronoun. Like so:

א   "**Eu** não irei com a minha mãe às compras. **Ela** gosta de ir sozinha. ↶ I won't go shopping with my mother. She likes to go alone."

Next, we will see what happens if we want to substitute a noun that is the object of the phrase, and not the subject. So, we can be talking about the direct object pronouns or indirect object pronouns. The difference between these two is quite easy to understand and will establish what role pronouns play in a sentence. Knowing what each group is all about will help you understand what the sentence means and what it is telling you—what is the function of each word and how they all connect. Let's get to it then.

The **direct object** category comprises ten pronouns:

א   "ME" ↶ in English it would translate to "ME"[30]

א   "TE" ↶ in English it would translate to "YOU"

א   "O" ↶ in English it would translate to "IT"

א   "A" ↶ in English it would translate to "IT"

א   "LHE" ↶ in English it would translate to "TO HIM/HER"

א   "NOS" ↶ in English it would translate to "US"

א   "VOS" ↶ in English it would translate to "YOU"

א   "OS" ↶ in English it would translate to "THEM"

---

30 They are written the same but sound different. While the English "ME" has the Portuguese "I" sound, with the open pronunciation, the Portuguese "ME" has an "E" sound, but a closed one.

ℵ   "AS" ↷ in English it would translate to "THEY"

ℵ   "LHES" ↷ in English it would translate to "TO THEM"

The **indirect object** category comprises eight pronouns:

ℵ   "ME" ↷ in English it would translate to "ME"

ℵ   "TE" ↷ in English it would translate to "YOU"

ℵ   "LHE" ↷ in English it would translate to "TO HIM/HER"

ℵ   "NOS" ↷ in English it would translate to "US"

ℵ   "VOS" ↷ in English it would translate to "YOU"

ℵ   "LHES" ↷ in English it would translate to "TO THEM"

The difference between these two groups of pronouns is, apparently, not much. However, depending on the function they are performing within a phrase, you can easily identify and separate them. The direct object pronouns will be achieved or lead the following specific questions: "O QUÊ? ↷ WHAT?" and "QUEM? ↷ WHO?"

On the other hand, with the indirect object pronouns, you will get to the questions "A QUEM?" and "PARA QUEM?" that in English translates to "TO WHOM?"

Let's see some examples and ask some questions to make the subject clearer.

ℵ   "Daniela vai dar a bola. ↷ Daniela is going to give the ball."

Who is going to give something? Daniela. **What** is Daniela going to give? A ball. So, we could substitute these two nouns for their pronouns, which belong to the direct object category. Like so:

ℵ   "**Ela** vai dá-**la**. ↷ She is going to give it."

Now, let's a look at another example:

ℵ   "Eu desobedeço aos meus pais. ↷ I disobey my parents."

Who doesn't obey? Me. To *whom*? My parents. You can see that the sentence already has the personal pronoun substituting the subject of the sentence (EU ↝ ME, instead of the subject's name), but we can also substitute the noun "PAIS ↝ PARENTS" for an indirect object pronoun. Like so:

> ℵ   "Eu desobedeço-**lhes**. ↝ I disobey them."

Now, the only thing left to do is figure out how to insert the pronouns in a sentence. How do we add the pronouns like we did in those examples given above? The good news is that the rules we are going to see next apply to both direct and indirect object pronouns. That makes things easier.

So, the first rule to know, which applies to most cases, is that we insert the pronoun after the verb, separated by the verb by a hyphen. So, for instance, the sentence:

> ℵ   "Eu comi a banana ontem. ↝ I ate the banana yesterday."

would turn into:

> ℵ   "Eu comi-**a** ontem. ↝ I ate it yesterday."

Even though the previous rule is the most frequent, there are a few situations in which the pronoun needs to be placed before the verb, or there is a contraction between words, or in some cases, we have to add a little something, and in others, we even have to mix direct and indirect object pronouns in the same word. It probably sounds harder than it actually is, so let's jump right in with no fear.

> ℵ   **When the verb ends IN "R," "S," or "Z"**
> ℵ   **When the verb ends with an "M"**
> ℵ   **The presence of both direct and indirect object pronouns**
> ℵ   **When there is an adverb**
> ℵ   **In a negative sentence**
> ℵ   **In a question**

ℵ   **When there is a relative pronoun**

ℵ   **When there is a preposition**

Let's take a look at what happens in each case.

ℵ   <u>**When the verb ends IN "R," "S," or "Z"**</u>

When the last letters of the verb are the ones mentioned, they get cut off, and you add an "L" to the beginning of the pronouns "O" or "A" (or "OS" or "AS" if it's in the plural form). For instance, let's take the first example given about the direct object pronouns:

     ℵ   "Daniela vai dar a bola. ↶ Daniela is going to give the ball."

"Ela vai dá-*la*. ↶ She is going to give it."

     ℵ   "Ele fez bolos. ↶ He baked cakes."

"Ele fê-*los*. ↶ He baked them."

ℵ   <u>**When the verb ends with an "M"**</u>

When the sentence has a verb that ends with an "M," i.e., a nasal sound, we have to keep the verb the same, but add an "N" to the pronoun. That happens because the sound of the verb ending in "M" with the "O" or "A" right after could end up being confusing. So, for instance:

     ℵ   "Eles cantam a canção muito bem. ↶ They sing the song very well."

"Eles cantam-*na* muito bem. ↶ They sing it very well."

ℵ   <u>**The presence of both direct and indirect object pronouns**</u>

Sometimes both direct and indirect objects are found in a sentence. To substitute the nouns for pronouns in this situation you need to mix both pronouns that are going to be used together.

     ℵ   "Eu dei a minha roupa à Inês ↶ I gave my clothes to Inês."

"Eu dei-*lha*. ↶ I gave it to her."

     ℵ   "Tu vendeste-me os livros. ↶ You sold the books to me."

"Tu vendeste-*mos*. ↵ You sold them to me."

So, in the first sentence, we can ask the following questions: *Who* is giving something? I am—"EU" is substituting the subject's name. Giving *what?* The clothes. In Portuguese, we are dealing with a feminine word, as you can see indicated by the feminine definite article that precedes it—"A ROUPA." So, when substituting it for a pronoun, we have to use "A." To *whom?* Inês. Up until here, we were dealing with direct object pronouns. However, this last question gives us the answer that will lead us to the correct indirect object pronoun, which is "LHE." Since we have to insert both "LHE" and "A" after the verb, they blend, creating "LHA."

The same logic works for the second example given, but now with the direct object pronoun "OS," and the indirect object pronoun "ME" since "you" (who?) sold the books (what?) to me (to whom?).

ℵ   When there is an adverb

When the sentence has an adverb, the rule changes completely. In the previous cases, the pronoun is inserted in the sentence after the verb. When there is an adverb in the sentence, modifying the verb, the adjective, or the adverb itself, the pronoun is instead inserted before the verb. Let's see a few examples, using the adverbs "JÁ ↵ ALREADY" and "TALVEZ ↵ MAYBE."

ℵ   "Ela já ofereceu o livro ao Miguel. ↵ She has already offered the book to Miguel."

"Ela já *lhe* ofereceu o livro. ↵ She has already offered him the book."

ℵ   "Talvez coma sopa. ↵ I might eat soup."

"Talvez *a* coma. ↵ I might eat it."

ℵ   In a negative sentence

If we are facing a negative sentence, the solution is the same as the last one you just saw. The pronoun is inserted before the verb. Like so:

ℵ "Tu não telefonaste à Tia Maria. ↪ You didn't call Tia Maria."

"Tu não ***lhe*** telefonaste. ↪ You didn't call her."

ℵ **In a question**

When it comes to sentences that are questions, the same rule you just saw applies once again. Let's see an example:

ℵ "Quem é que chamou os bombeiros? ↪ Who called the firemen?"

"Quem é que ***os*** chamou? ↪ Who called them?

ℵ **When there is a relative pronoun**[31]

When there is a relative pronoun in the sentence, the pronoun is inserted before the verb as well. It is getting easier by the "scroll," isn't it?

ℵ "Eu quero que faças os teus trabalhos de casa. ↪ I want you to do your homework."

"Eu quero que ***os*** faças. ↪ I want you to make it."

ℵ **When there is a preposition**

Finally, when there is a preposition in the sentence, we apply the same process we have been going through in these last situations. The pronoun is put before the verb. Like so:

ℵ "A avó disse aos seus netos para levarem guarda-chuva. ↪ The grandmother told her grandchildren to take an umbrella."

"A avó disse-lhes para ***o*** levarem. ↪ The grandmother told them to tacke it."

---

31 A relative pronoun represents nouns that were mentioned previously in a sentence and with which the relative pronoun is connected–just like what the word "WHICH" does in English, and did in this very sentence.

א Demonstrative pronouns

The case with the demonstrative pronouns is equal to what happens with the possessive pronouns. They exist not only to indicate the position of an object in place or time but also to substitute the noun while doing it. Let's see the examples we saw for the demonstrative determiners being used in a sentence, and some answers with demonstrative **pronouns**:

> א "<u>Esta</u> comida é óptima. Para mim, **esta** é melhor. ↶ This food is great. To me, this one is better."

> א "Dá-me esse livro. **Este** ou **aquele**? ↶ Give me that book. This or that one?"

> א "Não é ***esse***, é aquele livro ao fundo da prateleira. ↶ It isn't *that* one, it's the one by the end of the shelf."

Did you notice that in the last sentence, nothing was added? The previous sentences were the same examples given a few pages earlier, in the demonstrative determiners section, but a sentence with an example of a demonstrative possessive had to be added. In the last sentence, however, the sentence needs no additions. That is because it already has a demonstrative determiner. The first "ESSE" is referring to the book but substituting the noun, which only comes after the demonstrative determiner "AQUELE."

א Possessive pronouns

Finally, we have the possessive pronouns. The possessive pronouns are the possessive determiners you already studied a few pages earlier. However, they now are used differently. So, when facing a possessive determiner, we are dealing with a word that adds information about to whom something belongs, about who owns something. Nonetheless, if a word that indicates possession, completely substitutes the noun, it is then a possessive pronoun. Again, like with the demonstrative pronouns, let's take the examples we saw in the possessive determiners section and use possessive **pronouns** in a different situation. See the difference:

א   "Aquela[32] é a minha casa. Qual[33] é a **tua**? ↶ That is my house. Which one is yours?"

א   "A tua caneta é azul. A **minha** é verde. ↶ Your pen is blue. Mine is green."

א   "O vinho é nosso! Ou será **vosso**? ↶ The wine is ours! Or is it yours?"

א   "As cadeiras não são vossas. São **suas** ↶ The chairs are not yours. They are theirs."

Prepositions

Prepositions are words used to connect two parts of a sentence. They are never used by themselves because of that—their purpose is to establish the connection, the relationship between the two parts of a phrase, that are dependent and might mean something different without an element that ties them together. Let's see a few examples to understand better what this is all about:

Precedent	Preposition	Subsequent
Vou (I'm going)	**A** (To)	Paris
Chegarei (I will arrive)	**A** (On)	Tempo (Time)
Estado (State)	**De** (Of)	Espírito [34](Mind)
Chorei (I cried)	**De** (Of)	Dor (Pain)

---

32 Can you identify what "AQUELA" is? Is it a pronoun or determiner? That's right—it's a demonstrative pronoun! It substitutes the noun in the sentence.

33 We are not going to study the interrogative pronouns, but that is one example. It basically corresponds to the interrogative determiners, following the same logic we have been seeing—it substitutes the noun.

34 "Espírito" literally means "spirit," but the expression is more adequately translated into the known English expression "state of mind." Note that if there were no preposition—the "de" or "of" in the English version—the expression would not be or mean the same, even though both words can exist by themselves in a sentence. It is now, hopefully, clear that a preposition's function is to link words in a sentence to create a new meaning.

There are simple prepositions and compound prepositions. In this book, we will only focus on simple prepositions and what their function in a phrase usually is. They are:

- א A
- א APÓS
- א ATÉ
- א COM
- א CONTRA
- א DE
- א DESDE
- א EM
- א ENTRE
- א PARA
- א POR
- א SEM
- א SOB
- א SOBRE

Let's take a look at what role each preposition can play within a sentence.

א Preposition "A"

"A" generally indicates movement, in space or time, or it can indicate a situation, in space or time. Very frequently, you will see the contraction of this preposition with the definite article "O."

- א "Eu vou **a** Espanha. ↵ I'm going to Spain."

- א "Daqui **a** uma semana. ↵ In a week."

- א "O meu gato adormeceu **ao** meu lado. ↵ My cat fell asleep by my side."

- א "**A** 9 de Setembro tenho uma consulta. ↵ I have an appointment on September 9."

Notice that in the third sentence, we have "AO" instead of just "A." This is because when a definite article follows the preposition "A," they get together to form one word, which is itself a preposition, born of that contraction. However, what if the definite article that follows the preposition "A" is an "A"? Then, we signal it by adding the diacritical mark (´). Like so:

ℵ   "Vou comer fruta **à** sobremesa. ↩ I'm going to eat fruit for dessert."

ℵ   Preposition "Após"

"APÓS" indicates consequence, something after something, like the word "AFTER."

ℵ   "**Após** meia hora, chegámos. ↩ After half an hour, we arrived."

ℵ   "**Após** alguns segundos, parei. ↩ After a few seconds, I stopped."

ℵ   Preposition "Até"

"ATÉ" indicates the approximation of a limit, just like "TO," "UP TO," "BY," and "UNTIL" can indicate sometimes.

ℵ   "Ele foi **até** ao quarto. ↩ He went to the room."

ℵ   "Eu sei contar **até** dez. ↩ I know how to count up to ten."

ℵ   "Os resultados estarão prontos **até** amanhã. ↩ The results will be ready by tomorrow."

ℵ   "O prazo é **até** ao último segundo do dia. ↩ The deadline is until the last second of the day."

ℵ   Preposition "Com"

"COM" indicates addition, association, company, and so on, just like the word "WITH" does.

ℵ   "Nós vamos **com** eles às compras. ↩ We are going shopping with them."

ℵ   "**Com** um dia assim, temos que ir à praia. ↩ With a day like this, we have to go to the beach."

ℵ   "Eu quero pão **com** queijo. ↩ I want bread with cheese."

ℵ Preposition "Contra"

"CONTRA" expresses, much like the word "AGAINST," an idea of two things directed towards one another. It also translates to the word "VERSUS."

ℵ   "Eu joguei **contra** o João. ↵ I played against John."

ℵ   "Eu encostei o meu corpo **contra** o seu. ↵ I pressed my body against his."

ℵ   "Eu **contra** ti. ↵ Me versus you."

ℵ Preposition "De"

"DE" indicates the movement away from something, or the origin of that movement or that something, much like the word "FROM."

ℵ   "Vieste **de** longe? ↵ Did you come from far?"

ℵ   "O pássaro despareceu **de** um momento para o outro[35]. ↵ Then the bird disappeared."

ℵ   "O barulho vem **de** fora. ↵ The noise comes from outside."

ℵ   "É sal **do** mar. ↵ It's salt from the sea."

ℵ   "A areia é **da** praia. ↵ The sand is from the beach."

You may have noticed, once again, that in the last two sentences, the preposition changed to "DO" and "DA." This is because the preposition must match the gender of the word.

Preposition "Desde"

"DESDE" expresses the movement away from something, much like "DE," but with some emphasis on that origin. It translates most times to "SINCE," but it can also be expressed by "FROM."

ℵ   "**Desde** a semana passada. ↵ Since last week."

ℵ   "Eu consigo ver as montanhas **desde** a minha casa. ↵ I can see the mountains from my house."

---

35 Literally, "from one moment to the other." It means that something happened really fast, with no warning.

ℵ Preposition "Em"

"EM" can be indicative of time, space, or mode.

ℵ   "Eu estou **em** casa. ↶ I'm at home."

ℵ   "De vez **em** quando, vemos uma raposa por aqui. ↶ Once in a while, we see a fox around here."

ℵ   "**Em** Fevereiro faço anos. ↶ In February, it's my birthday."

ℵ   "Eu vou pagar **em** dinheiro. ↶ I will pay in cash."

This preposition can also come before a definite article. In that case, if the article is "O," the preposition turns into "NO"; if instead, the article is "A," then the preposition turns into "NA."

ℵ   "As minhas coisas estão **no** carro. ↶ My things are in the car."

ℵ   "Elas não acreditam **nas** vacinas. ↶ They don't believe in the vaccines."

ℵ Preposition "Entre"

"ENTRE" indicates the position between two limits. "BETWEEN" is actually the preposition that translates this same idea in English.

ℵ   "Eu estou **entre** a espada e a parede[36]. ↶ Between a rock and a hard place/Between the devil and the deep blue sea."

ℵ   "Não há nada **entre** nós. ↶ There is nothing between us."

ℵ Preposition "Para"

"PARA" expresses movement toward a limit, an end-goal, an objective within the sentence. It is similar to the preposition "A," but it differs from it because it implies a bigger emphasis on the starting

---

36 Literally, it would mean "between a sword and the wall." Even though it will have to do, the translation written in the text is not quite perfect since the Portuguese expression means that there is no available choice. In contrast, the expression in English is more related to having to choose between an equally unpleasant outcome.

point and direction, instead of focusing more on the idea of the movement ending.

- ℵ   "Eu vou **para** Berlim. ↪ I am going to Berlin."

- ℵ   "**Para** mim, isso não faz sentido. ↪ To me, that doesn't make sense."

- ℵ   "A gente está a ir **para** a missa. ↪ The crowd is going to the church."

ℵ Preposition "Por"

The preposition "POR" indicates the extension between limits, across time, space, and other concepts. For instance:

- ℵ   "Vou ficar preso **por** seis meses. ↪ I'm going to be in jail for six months."

- ℵ   "Vou contar moeda **por** moeda. ↪ I'm going to count coin by coin."

- ℵ   "Vamos viajar **por** Coimbra. ↪ We are going to travel by Coimbra."

Like what happened with the prepositions "A," "DE," and "EM," when there is a definite article after the preposition, we contract both words. The preposition "POR" is the one that changes the most, however: when there is the definite article "A" after, it changes to "PELA"; when there is the definite article "O" after it, the preposition changes to "PELO." Let's see those applied to a sentence:

- ℵ   "Saímos **pela** madrugada. ↪ We leave by dawn."

- ℵ   "Passei **pelo** supermercado para comprar água. ↪ I went by the supermarket to buy water."

ℵ Preposition "Sem"

"SEM" indicates the lack of something, much like the preposition "WITHOUT." It is the opposite of "COM."

ℵ "**Sem** ti, a vida não faz sentido. ⤻ Without you, life makes no sense."

ℵ "Eu quero uma salada **sem** tomate, por favor. ⤻ I want a salad with no tomato, please."

ℵ **Preposition "Sob"**

"SOB" indicates an inferior position, just like "UNDER," "UNDERNEATH," or "BENEATH."

ℵ "O garfo está **sob** a mesa. ⤻ The fork is underneath the table."

ℵ "O país está **sob** a liderança de um governo socialista. ⤻ The country is under the leadership of a socialist government."

ℵ "**Sob** o sol. ⤻ Underneath the sun."

ℵ **Preposition "Sobre"**

"SOBRE" is the opposite of the preposition "SOB," indicating a position of superiority, just like the english words "ON," "UPON," "ABOUT," or "OVER."

ℵ "O garfo está **sobre** a mesa. ⤻ The fork is over the table."

ℵ "Vamos falar **sobre** política. ⤻ Let's talk about politics."

ℵ "Vou reflectir **sobre** isso. ⤻ I'm going to reflect upon that."

ℵ "Ele escreveu um livro **sobre** desporto. ⤻ He wrote a book on sports."

Adjectives

Adjectives exist to give an attribute to a noun. In Portuguese, they must agree in number and gender with the noun they are describing. So, it is essential to notice and identify in which gender the substantive is–masculine or feminine–so you know how to write the adjective accordingly. The same things apply to number. The adjective must be in accordance with the noun in number—singular or plural. You will see in more detail how to do this in the next section.

For now, check out the table below in which we start with some nouns and transform them into adjectives:

Noun	Masculine	Feminine	Plural
Beleza (Beauty)	Belo (Beautiful)	Bela	Belos/as
Rapidez (Quickness)	Rápido (Quick)	Rápida	Rápidos/as
Altura (Height)	Alto (Tall)	Alta	Alto/as
Gordura (Fatness)	Gordo (Fat)	Gorda	Gordo/as
Bondade (Kindness)	Bom (Kind)	Boa	Bons/Boas
Fealdade (Ugliness)	Feio (Ugly)	Feia	Feios/as
Sabor (Taste)	Saboroso (Tasty)	Saborosa	Saborosos/as
Maldade (Badness, wickedness, evilness)	Mau (Bad, wicked, evil)	Má	Maus/Más
Inteligência (Intelligence)	Inteligente (Intelligent)	Inteligente	Inteligentes

Even though most adjectives that end in "O" need to change the ending to an "A" to be in the feminine form, some adjectives do not follow this rule. Some are uniform and maintain the same letters in either form—like the adjective "INTELIGENTE"; others are irregular, and have to completely change their ending, like "MAU ↶ MÁ," or "BOM ↶ BOA." Since there is no rule to apply to those situations, you just have to read, write, and practice!

As for the variation in number, you probably noticed that in almost every case, we just needed to add an "S" to express the plural form. The only exception was with the adjective "BOM," which turned into "BONS." That happens because, in Portuguese, we cannot ever have an "M" before an "S." So, with every word that ends in "M," we add an "S" to make it plural, but change the "M" to "N." But more of that in a bit! Now, off to the variation of gender.

Adverbs

An adverb is a word that modifies the verb, the adjective, or another adverb. It never modifies a noun. It basically expresses or illustrates the circumstances in which the verbal action occurs. Let's see how an adverb can modify each one of the classes of words mentioned above.

"A Professora <u>ensinou</u> *pacientemente* a matéria. ↶ The teacher taught the subject patiently."

"Ele era *extremamente* <u>alto</u>. ↶ He was extremely tall."

"Havia *muito* <u>poucas</u> bananas. ↶ There weren't many bananas."

See that in the first sentence, the adverb "PACIENTEMENTE" modifies the verb "ENSINAR," specifying how it is being done. In the second sentence, the adverb "EXTREMAMENTE" changes the adjective "ALTO," adding another detail to the description of the man. Finally, in the third sentence, the adverb "MUITO" changes the adverb "POUCO," functioning as an emphasis on the low number of bananas.

Adverbs can do these modifications in several different ways—seven, to be specific. These are the categories of adverbs:

א   Adverbs of affirmation

א Adverbs of denial

א Adverbs of doubt

א Adverbs of exclusivity

א Adverbs of mode or manner

א Adverbs of place

א Adverbs of quantity or intensity

א Adverbs of time

Even though the names of the categories are pretty self-explanatory, let's go through each one and look at a few examples.

א Adverbs of affirmation

The adverbs of affirmation are inserted in sentences to make an affirmation.

א Certamente ↶ Certainly

א Decerto ↶ Surely

א Efectivamente ↶ Effectively

א Realmente ↶ Really

א Sim ↶ Yes

א Adverbs of denial

The adverbs of denial are inserted in sentences to deny something.

א Jamais ↶ Ever

א Não ↶ No

א Nunca ↶ Never

א Tampouco ↶ Nor, neither

א Adverbs of doubt

The adverbs of doubt indicate doubt or a question within a sentence.

א Possivelmente ↶ Possibly

א Provavelmente ↶ Probably

א Quiçá ↶ Perhaps

א Talvez ↶ Maybe

א

א Adverbs of exclusivity

The adverbs of exclusivity express an idea of exclusion of some elements within the sentence.

- א   Apenas ⌐ Only, just
- א   Excepto ⌐ Except, save
- א   Só ⌐ Only
- א   Unicamente ⌐ Uniquely

א Adverbs of mode or manner

The adverbs of manner express the mode or manner in which the action occurs. It is related to the question "COMO? ⌐ HOW?"

- א   Assim ⌐ Thus, therefore
- א   Bem ⌐ Well, right
- א   Mal ⌐ Badly
- א   Devagar ⌐ Slowly
- א   Facilmente ⌐ Easily
- א   Rapidamente ⌐ Quickly
- א   Lentamente ⌐ Slowly
- א   Cuidadosamente ⌐ Carefully

א Adverbs of place

The adverbs of place indicate where the action occurs. It is related to the question "ONDE? ⌐ WHERE?"

- א   Abaixo ⌐ Below
- א   Acima ⌐ Above
- א   Adentro ⌐ Inside
- א   Aí ⌐ There, then
- א   Além ⌐ Over there, beyond
- א   Ali ⌐ Over there, in there
- א   Algures ⌐ Somewhere
- א   Nenhures ⌐ Nowhere
- א   Aqui ⌐ Here

ℵ   Adverbs of quantity or intensity

The adverbs of quantity or intensity express the quantity or degree with which the verbal action occurs. It indicates how much, to what degree, or to what extent something is happening.

- ℵ   Bastante ↪ Quite, enough
- ℵ   Demais ↪ Too, too much
- ℵ   Demasiado ↪ Too, too much
- ℵ   Imenso ↪ A lot
- ℵ   Mais ↪ More, further, much
- ℵ   Menos ↪ Least
- ℵ   Muito ↪ Much, very, highly
- ℵ   Pouco ↪ Little
- ℵ   Quase ↪ Almost
- ℵ   Suficientemente ↪ Sufficiently, enough

ℵ   Adverbs of time

The adverbs of time indicate the moment when the action occurs, or how often. It is associated with the question "QUANDO? ↪ WHEN?"

- ℵ   Afinal ↪ After all
- ℵ   Agora ↪ Now
- ℵ   Amanhã ↪ Tomorrow
- ℵ   Antes ↪ Before
- ℵ   Depois ↪ After
- ℵ   Frequentemente ↪ Frequently, often
- ℵ   Já ↪ Already, now, yet
- ℵ   Sempre ↪ Always

You probably noticed that many adverbs have the ending "MENTE," much like the adverbs in English have the ending "LY." That could be an easy trick to remind yourself how to generally identify adverbs within sentences, and also how to create them from adjectives.

Accordance with gender

The variation in gender is, generally, something that is very easy to solve. Most of the time, the "O" at the end of a noun indicates that the word is masculine; an "A" is feminine. There is no neutral gender—a noun will always be either masculine or feminine, even if there is no "O" or "A" at the end. In those cases, the article before the noun might do the trick. Remember that the determiners and the adjectives have to agree with the gender of the noun. Let's see some examples:

- ℵ **A** minh**a** caix**a**. ↶ My box.
- ℵ Aquel**a** camis**a**. ↶ That shirt.
- ℵ **O** chã**o** é pret**o**. ↶ The floor is black.
- ℵ Ess**a** bol**a** é redond**a**. ↶ That ball is round.

We have already seen the feminine forms of the determiners. However, with the nouns and adjectives, usually, to change the gender of one word to the other, you just have to change the "O" into "A," or vice-versa. That applies to nouns whose gender may vary. Evidently, when we are talking, for instance, about a "MESA ↶ TABLE," which is a feminine noun, we cannot change its gender. The gender generally changes when we are referring to people or animals. So, with:

- ℵ <u>**Nouns ending in "O"**</u>
  - ℵ   Aluno/a ↶ Student
  - ℵ   Gato/a ↶ Cat
  - ℵ   Lobo/a ↶ Wolf, she-wolf
  - ℵ   Menino/a ↶ Boy/girl

This is, obviously, a rule with many exceptions. Several nouns that end in "A" are masculine, and several ones that don't end in "A" are feminine. For instance:

- ℵ   **O** saca-rolh**as** ↶ Bottle opener
- ℵ   **O** Poet**a** ↶ Poet
- ℵ   **Um** pijam**a** ↶ Pajamas

℣   **A** aguarden<u>te</u>[37] ↶ Brandy

℣   **Uma** alfac<u>e</u> ↶ Lettuce

℣   **A** dinami<u>te</u> ↶ Dynamite

℣ Nouns ending in "ÃO"

When it comes to nouns ending in "ÃO," which is masculine, their feminine form can be achieved by taking away the "ÃO" and adding "Ã," "OA," or "ONA." Let's see some examples:

℣   Campeão - Campe**ã** ↶ Champion

℣ Cirurgião - Cirurgi**ã** ↶ Surgeon

℣   Patrão - Patr**oa** ↶ Boss

℣   Leão - Le**oa** ↶ Lion - Lioness

℣   Cabeção - Cabeç**ona** ↶ Somebody with a big head

℣   Pobretão - Pobret**ona** ↶ Somebody who is really poor

℣ Nouns ending with a consonant

With most of the nouns that end with a consonant, usually a masculine form, we just have to add an "A" to the end of the word, while maintaining the ending.

℣   Camponês - Camponesa ↶ Peasant

℣   Cantor - Cantora ↶ Singer

℣   Condutor - Condutora ↶ Driver

℣   Freguês - Freguesa ↶ Citizen, customer

℣   Professor - Professora ↶ Professor, teacher[38]

℣   Senador - Senadora ↶ Senator

℣   Senhor - Senhora ↶ Sir - Madam

℣   Vendedor - Vendedora ↶ Salesman - Saleswoman

---

37 "Aguardente" is a very strong Portuguese drink that looks like water but smells and tastes like fire. After all, it literally means "burning/ardent water."

38 Even though in English, these words describe different realities, in Portuguese, both translate to "Professor" or "Professora."

However, some nouns that end in "OR" don't change to "ORA" to make it a feminine noun; instead, they change to "EIRA," taking out the "OR" at the end of the noun. Like so:

ℵ   Cantador - Cantadeira ↝ Singer

ℵ   Lavador - Lavadeira ↝ Washer (either a man or a woman)

ℵ   **Nouns ending in "E"**

Most nouns that end in "E" just need to switch this "E" for an "A" to get the feminine form:

ℵ   Mestre - Mestra ↝ Master

ℵ   Monge - Monja ↝ Monk

ℵ   **Nouns ending in "EL"**

When it comes to nouns ending in "EL," our job is easy. They are almost always masculine. Take a look at a few examples:

ℵ   O pincel ↝ The paintbrush

ℵ   O mel ↝ The honey

ℵ   O papel ↝ The paper

However, there are some exceptions. Here is a list of words that do not follow any rules and that you should try to memorize:

ℵ   Actor - Actriz ↝ Actor - Actress

ℵ   Boi - Vaca ↝ Ox - Cow

ℵ   Conde - Condessa ↝ Count - Countess

ℵ   Duque - Duquesa ↝ Duke - Duchess

ℵ   Genro - Sogra ↝ Son-in-law - Mother-in-law

ℵ   Herói - Heroína ↝ Hero - Heroine

ℵ   Homem - Mulher ↝ Man - Woman

ℵ   Imperador - Imperatriz ↝ Emperor - Empress

ℵ   Pai - Mãe ↝ Father - Mother

ℵ   Poeta - Poetisa ↝ Poet - Poetess

ℵ   Sultão - Sultana ↝ Sultan - Sultana

As for the adjectives, though many words that have the same endings as the nouns have the same rules, there are some exceptions. Let's take a look at a few specificities within the class of adjectives in terms of gender variation.

ℵ Adjectives ending in "U," "ÊS," and "OR"

With adjectives ending in those three ways, we just need to add an "A."

- ℵ   Cru - Crua ↵ Raw
- ℵ   Nu - Nua ↵ Naked
- ℵ   Francês - Francesa ↵ French
- ℵ   Inglês - Inglesa ↵ English
- ℵ   Conservador - Conservadora ↵ Conservative
- ℵ   Encantador - Encantadora ↵ Charming, enchanting

ℵ Adjectives ending in "ÃO"

When adjectives end in "ÃO," they sometimes change to "Ã"; other times to "ONA" to achieve the feminine gender.

- ℵ   São - Sã ↵ Healthy
- ℵ   Chorão - Chorona ↵ Somebody that cries a lot

ℵ Adjectives ending in "EU"

Finally, when adjectives end in "EU," we just have to change the "EU" to "EIA." Like so:

- ℵ   Europeu - Europeia ↵ European
- ℵ   Hebreu - Hebreia ↵ Hebrew
- ℵ   Plebeu - Plebeia ↵ Plebeian, commoner

Accordance to number

Now let's see how to put singular nouns and adjectives into their plural forms. We will analyze six different sets of words that follow a rule when changing into the plural form. They are:

- ℵ Words ending in a vowel our diphthongs
- ℵ Words ending in "AL" and "UL"
- ℵ Words ending in "EL" and "OL"
- ℵ Words ending in "R," "Z," or "N"
- ℵ Words ending in "ÃO"
- ℵ Compound nouns

ℵ <u>Words ending in "A," "E," "O," "I," "U," and nasal vowel</u>

Let's start with words that end with a vowel—usually, all you need is to add an "S" at the end.

- ℵ Mesa - Mesas ↳ Table - Tables
- ℵ Mochila - Mochilas ↳ Backpack - Backpacks
- ℵ Estante - Estantes ↳ Bookcase - Bookcases
- ℵ Mãe - Mães ↳ Mother - Mothers
- ℵ Lei - Leis ↳ Law - Laws
- ℵ Javali - Javalis ↳ Boar - Boars
- ℵ Tinteiro - Tinteiros ↳ Toner - Toners
- ℵ Saco - Sacos ↳ Bag - Bags
- ℵ Pau - Paus ↳ Stick - Sticks
- ℵ Peru - Perus ↳ Turkey - Turkeys

With words that end with *nasal vowels* (to make a nasal sound with "A," "E," "I," "O," and "U" at the end of the word, you add the letter "M"), you add the "S" but have to change the "M" to an "N" because, as you saw in the adjectives section, you cannot have "MS" in Portuguese. So, this is what should happen:

- ℵ Bem - Bens ↳ Good - Goods
- ℵ Som - Sons ↳ Sound - Sounds
- ℵ Atum - Atuns ↳ Tuna

ℵ <u>Words ending in "AL," "EL," "OL," and "UL"</u>

With these words, we just need to get rid of the "L" and add an "IS" instead.

- ℵ   Animal - Animais ↝ Animal - Animals
- ℵ   Paul - Pauis ↝ Bog - Bogs
- ℵ   Níquel - Níqueis ↝ Nickel - Nickels
- ℵ   Álcool - Álcoois ↝ Alcohol - Alcohols

ℵ   Words ending in "IL"

When we are facing words that end in "IL," we have to substitute the "L" for an "S." Like so:

- ℵ   Ardil - Ardis ↝ Trick - Tricks
- ℵ   Barril - Barris ↝ Barrel - Barrels
- ℵ   Covil - Covis ↝ Lair - Lairs

ℵ   Words ending in "R", "Z" or "N"

When we find words that end in "R," "Z," or "N," we just need to add an "ES" to the end of the word. Like so:

- ℵ   Mar - Mares ↝ Sea - Seas
- ℵ   Colher - Colheres ↝ Spoon - Spoons
- ℵ   Rapaz - Rapazes ↝ Boy - Boys
- ℵ   Cruz - Cruzes ↝ Cross - Crosses
- ℵ   Abdómen - Abdómenes ↝ Abdomen - Abdomens
- ℵ   Cânon - Cânones ↝ Canon - Canons

ℵ   Words ending in "ÃO"

Now, we are going to deal with words that end in "ÃO." With these types of words, there are three options in the plural form: it can end in "ÕES" or "ÃES" instead of "ÃO," or an "S" is just added at the end. There is no rule or criteria to use. You really just have to memorize it. However, the most common one is "ÕES," so if in doubt, just go for it and risk it. You will definitely make a mistake that many Portuguese natives, who have been studying this and hearing the language their whole lives, sometimes still make!

א   Balão - Balões ↶ Balloon - Balloons

א   Botão - Botões ↶ Button - Buttons

א   Canção - Canções ↶ Song - Songs

א   Coração - Corações ↶ Heart - Hearts

א   Cão - Cães ↶ Dog - Dogs

א   Pão - Pães ↶ Bread - Breads

א   Catalão - Catalães ↶ Catalan - Catalans

א   Guardião - Guardiães ↶ Guardian - Guardians

א   Cidadão - Cidadãos ↶ Citizen - Citizens

א   Mão - Mãos ↶ Hand - Hands

א   Bênção - Bênçãos ↶ Blessing - Blessings

א   Órfão - Órfãos ↶ Orphan - Orphans

א Compound nouns

Finally, the hard part—the compound nouns. Compounds nouns are nouns composed of two words. Surprising, isn't it? More surprising is how to understand the plural of the compound nouns. It is not always easy. Let's dive in.

א   Compound nouns with no hyphen

Firstly, we have the compound nouns that are composed of words that are together with no hyphen. The plural of these words is easy: we just need to add an "S" to the end of the word. Like so:

א   Aguardente - Aguardentes ↶ Brandy - Brandies

א   Clarabóia - Clarabóias ↶ Skylight - Skylights

א   Malmequer - Malmequeres ↶ Daisy - Daisies

א   Pontapé - Pontapés ↶ Kick - Kicks

א   Compound nouns with a hyphen

When we are facing words that have a hyphen, the plural can be applied to both words, to the first or the second word. See the examples below:

א   Couve-flor - <u>Couves-flores</u> ↩ Cauliflower - Cauliflowers

א   Obra-prima - <u>Obras-primas</u> ↩ Masterpiece - Masterpieces

א   Navio-escola - Navios-escola ↩ Training ship - Training ships

א   Grão-mestre - Grão-<u>mestres</u> ↩ Grandmaster - Grandmasters

א   Guarda-marinha – <u>Guardas-marinhas</u> ↩ Coast guard – Coast guards

א   Guarda-roupa - Guarda-<u>roupas</u> ↩ Wardrobe - Wardrobes

However, there are some details we can pay attention to and also apply a few set of rules to that will help us. So:

a) if the first word of the noun is a verb or an invariable word[39], and the second word is a noun or an adjective, only the second word changes to the plural form:

א   Guarda-chuva - Guarda-chuvas ↩ Umbrella - Umbrellas

א   Vice-presidente – Vice-presidentes ↩ Vice president – Vice presidents

א   Bate-boca – Bate-bocas ↩ Squabble – Squabbles

א   Abaixo-assinado - Abaixo-assinados ↩ Petition - Petitions

א   Grão-duque – Grão-duques ↩ Grand duke - Grand dukes

---

39 An invariable word is a word that does not change in number or gender.

b) if the two words are connected by a preposition, only the first word turns into the plural form:

ℵ   Chapéu-de-sol – Chapéus-de-sol ↶ Sunhat – Sunhats

ℵ   Pão-de-ló[40] – Pães-de-ló ↶ Sponge cake – Sponge cakes

ℵ   Pé-de-cabra – Pés-de-cabra ↶ Crowbar – Crowbars

c) if the second word of the noun is a noun that works as a specific determiner[41], only the first word in the noun turns into the plural form as well:

ℵ   Decreto-lei – Decretos-lei ↶ Decree-law – Decree-laws

ℵ   Contrato-promessa – Contratos-promessa ↶ Pre-agreement – Pre-agreements

ℵ   Palavra-chave – Palavras-chave ↶ Password – Passwords

d) Finally, if the word is composed of two nouns, or of a noun and an adjective, both words turn into their respective plural. Like so:

ℵ   Carta-bilhete – Cartas-bilhetes ↶ Letter/note – Letters/notes

ℵ   Amor-perfeito – Amores-perfeitos ↶ Pansy – Pansies

ℵ   Pequeno-almoço – Pequenos-almoços ↶ Breakfast – Breakfasts

ℵ   Cidade-estado – Cidades-estados ↶ City State – City States

You are probably tired of nouns by now, but what about the adjectives? Well, the reason for the lack of attention concerning adjectives is that they follow the same rules as nouns. Nevertheless,

---

40 "Pão-de-ló" is a very traditional cake in Portugal. It is made of eggs, flour, and sugar—the secret is that it's undercooked, to the point that inside is super moist. Yummy!

41 It means it specifies what the first noun is or how it works or is applied.

and as always, there is an exception[42]. In the compound adjectives, like "Médico-cirúrgico ↶ Surgeon," only the second word, the one after the hyphen, turns into the plural form. So:

ℵ   Médico-cirúrgico – Médico-cirúgicos ↶ Surgeon – Surgeons

ℵ   Afro-asiático – Afro-asiáticos ↶ Afro-asian – Afro-asians

ℵ   Anglo-saxónico – Anglo-saxónicos ↶ Anglo-saxon – Anglo-saxons

Yet, there are exceptions to the exceptions. With the word "SURDO-MUDO ↶ DEAF-MUTE," for instance, the plural form is on both words.

---

42 As the Portuguese saying goes: "A excepção confirma a regra. ↶ The exception proves/confirms the rule."

#1 – Hora de Quiz!₄₃

1) Indicate to which class of nouns these words belong to:

Carro; pessoa; João; cidade; Lisboa; pinhal; generosidade; rapaz; aflição; turma; felicidade; América; alegria; formigueiro; casal; Mondego; rio; bondade; frota; pensamento.

2) Highlight the words that can be both proper and common nouns:

Luís; oliveira; porto; câmara; computador; escola; caderno; copo; Albufeira

3) Write the correct definite article—singular or plural, masculine or feminine—before the following words:

Carro; sapo; folha; árvore; corações; televisão; toalhas; sabonetes

4) Write the correct definite article—singular or plural, masculine or feminine—before the following words:

Mesas; borracha; afia; forno; quadros; saia; vela; filme

5) Identify the determiners in the sentences, and write down to which group they belong to:

---

43 "Quiz time!"

64

"Essa chave não é a minha chave. Alguém a roubou! ↳ That key is not my key. Somebody stole it!"

"Cada um de nós tem pouco para fazer. ↳ Each one of us hasn't got much to do."

"Aquele animal está muito perto de nós. ↳ That animal is very near to us."

"O vosso pai é sempre o mesmo palerma. ↳ Your dad is always the same dork."

"Eu não sei quem tu és. ↳ I don't know who you are."

6)   Underline the pronouns in the following sentences:

"Eu tenho uma bola azul. Vou dá-la à Mariana ↳ I have a blue ball. I'm going to give it to Mariana."

"Estás a ver as casas desta rua? Aquela é a minha. ↳ Are you seeing the houses in this street? That one is my own."

"A Catarina irá cozinhar o jantar. Ela cozinha muito bem. ↳ Catarina will cook dinner. She cooks very well."

7)   Insert prepositions to complete the sentences:

"Eu gosto _ aprender Português. ↳ I like learning Portuguese."

"O meu avô vai ___ hospital. ↳ My grandfather is going to the hospital."

"O meu cão está ___ casa_ meu vizinho. ↳ My dog is at my neighbor's house."

8)   Transform the nouns into adjectives and insert them in the following sentences:

"O meu pai é muito _____(gordura)."

"A água está ____(gelo)."

"Jogar basquetebol é muito _____(diversão)."

"Eu acho a escola _____(aborrecimento)."

9)   Write down these words according to the feminine gender:

Juiz; senhor; aluno; imperador; vendedor; actor; leitor; espanhol; português; pigmeu; infante; inspector; jornalista; embaixador; doente.

10)   Write these words in their plural form:

Mar; rapaz; pato; canção; escrivão; cristão; irmão; alemão; opinião; sótão; paredão; farol; móvel; animal; funil; fóssil; nuvem; jardim.

PART II: GRAMMAR[44]

44 The recommended song for this chapter is "O Cheiro dos Livros" by Cabeças no Ar.

67

Did you know that there are three big classes of verbs in Portuguese? The ones ending in "AR," the ones ending in "ER," and the ones ending in "IR." Assuming the verb we are facing is a regular verb[45], and depending on the ending we are dealing with, the conjugation of that verb will always be the same. This means that the stem of the verb continues being the same (the part of the verb that is left once you take the "AR," "ER," or "IR"), while you substitute the ending. Piece of cake, isn't it?[46]

---

45 Regular verbs are the ones that maintain the stem throughout the whole process of conjugation.

46 Or, in Portuguese, "É canja!" While it is the equivalent of the expression in the text, meaning that something is very easy to do, it literally means "It's broth!" More specifically, chicken broth, a very popular Portuguese soup, which is very easy to make—hence the saying.

Basic Portuguese Verbs

Below is a list of the twenty most used verbs in Portuguese. Some of them we will conjugate in three different tenses in the next section. Study them well and revisit this chapter—you will definitely need to use, hear, or read most (if not all) of these verbs, sooner or later.

א   Amar ᕁ (to) Love

א   Cantar ᕁ (to) Sing

א   Comer ᕁ (to) Eat

א   Dar ᕁ (to) Give

א   Dizer ᕁ (to) Say

א   Estar* ᕁ (to) Be

א   Estudar ᕁ (to) Study

א   Falar ᕁ (to) Speak

א   Fazer ᕁ (to) Do

א   Haver ᕁ (to) Exist

א   Ir ᕁ (to) Go

א   Olhar ᕁ (to) Look

א   Partir ᕁ (to) Break

א   Poder ᕁ Can

א   Pôr ᕁ (to) Put

ℵ   Querer ↩ (to) Want

ℵ   Ser* ↩ (to) Be

ℵ   Ter ↩ (to) Have

ℵ   Trazer ↩ (to) Bring

ℵ   Vir ↩ (to) Come

Note: The verbs "SER" and "ESTAR" translate to the verb "TO BE." However, while "SER" is used to talk about permanent, steady states that won't ever change, the verb "ESTAR" is, generally, used in states that are more likely to suffer changes. So, for instance, you would have to use the verb "SER" to talk about your personality, sexuality, or nationality.[47] The verb "ESTAR" would be reserved for those other things that might change throughout your life, like the weather or how you feel at a given day. So, for instance, you would say, "Eu *sou* Portuguesa ↩ I'm Portuguese," but say, "Eu **estou** em Portugal ↩ I am in Portugal."

Tenses

Now, let's get to the tenses and start conjugating verbs! Sounds fun, right? Don't worry, it is not as boring, nor as difficult, as you might think. As you now know, there are three classes of verbs. Again, we will keep the stem of the verb and change the ending, according to the tense that we are conjugating the verb in.

You will surely know the infinitive, so we will focus and study the Present tense, Past Simple tense, and Future Indicative Tense. These are the tenses that are most commonly used and fundamental to know and master to understand basic Portuguese.

---

47 To say that you are married, what verb would you use? Supposedly, being something that could change, the answer should be that you should use the verb "ESTAR." However, it is very common to say, "Eu sou casado/a ↩ I'm married" using the verb "SER" instead. And that happens because, a long time ago, when somebody got married, it was not supposed to be a temporary state, but last forever.

Keep in mind that the rules you are about to study only apply to the regular verbs. The irregular verbs are just that—irregular; they follow no rule. They basically obey nothing.

"AR" ending

Let's take the verb "ESTUDAR ↵ (TO) STUDY," for instance.

"ESTUDAR"	Present Tense	Past Simple	Future
Eu ↵ I	Estud-*o*	Estud-*ei*	Estudar-*ei*
Tu ↵ You	Estud-*as*	Estud-*aste*	Estudar-*ás*
Ele/Ela ↵ He/She	Estud-*a*	Estud-*ou*	Estudar-*á*
Nós ↵ We	Estud-*amos*	Estud-*ámos*	Estudar-
Vós ↵ You[48]	Estud-*ais*	Estud-*astes*	Estudar-*eis*
Eles/Elas ↵ They	Estud-*am*	Estudar-*am*	Estudar-*ão*

In the Present Tense, you just have to add the following endings to the stem of the verb: "O," "AS," "A," "AMOS," "AIS," and "AM."

In the Past Simple Tense, you just have to add the following endings to the stem of the verb: "EI," "ASTE," "OU," "ÁMOS," "AIS," and "AM."

In the Future Indicative Tense, you just have to add the following endings to the stem of the verb: "EI," "ÁS," "Á," "EMOS," "EIS," and "ÃO."

"ER" ending

---

[48] "VÓS" is a dated word. Instead, what is more frequently used is "VOCÊS." However, the verb after is conjugated in the third-person plural. Like so:

"Vós estudais muito – Vocês estudam muito. ↵ You study a lot."

Let's take the verb "COMER ↶ (TO) EAT," for instance.

"EAT"	Present Tense	Past Simple	Future
Eu ↶ I	Com-*o*	Com-*i*	Comer-*ei*
Tu ↶ You	Com-*es*	Com-*este*	Comer-*ás*
Ele/Ela ↶ He/She	Com-*e*	Com-*eu*	Comer-*á*
Nós ↶ We	Com-*emos*	Com-*emos*	Comer-*emos*
Vós ↶ You	Com-*eis*	Com-*estes*	Comer-*eis*
Eles/Elas ↶ They	Com-*em*	Comer-*am*	Comer-*ão*

In the Present Tense, you just have to add the following endings to the stem of the verb: "O," "ES," "E," "EMOS," "EIS," and "EM."

In the Past Simple Tense, you just have to add the following endings to the stem of the verb: "I," "ESTE," "EU," "EMOS," "ESTES," and "AM."

In the Future Indicative Tense, you just have to add the following endings to the stem of the verb: "EI," "ÁS," "Á," "EMOS," "EIS," and "ÃO."

"IR" ending

Let's take the verb "PARTIR ↪ (TO) BREAK," for instance.

"PARTIR"	**Present Tense**	**Past Simple**	**Future**
Eu ↪ I	Part-*o*	Part-*i*	Partir-*ei*
Tu ↪ You	Part-*es*	Part-*iste*	Partir-*ás*
Ele/Ela ↪ He/She	Part-*e*	Part-*iu*	Partir-*á*
Nós ↪ We	Part-*imos*	Part-*imos*	Partir-*emos*
Vós ↪ You	Part-*is*	Part-*istes*	Partir-*eis*
Eles/Elas ↪ They	Part-*em*	Partir-*am*	Partir-*ão*

In the Present Tense, you just have to add the following endings to the stem of the verb: "O," "ES," "E," "IMOS," "IS," and "EM."

In the Past Simple Tense, you just have to add the following endings to the stem of the verb: "I," "ISTE," "IU," "IMOS," "ISTES," and "AM."

In the Future Indicative Tense, you just have to add the following endings to the stem of the verb: "EI," "ÁS," "Á," "EMOS," "EIS," and "ÃO."

Irregular verbs + Exceptions

However, as mentioned, we have verbs that even though they belong in one of the three classes of verbs seen above, they actually do not. Confusing, right? This is because they are irregular verbs, exceptions with which we cannot follow the rules studied earlier. When those come before you, you just have to memorize them... Let's see an example of an irregular verb of each verb group, conjugated in the three tenses.

Starting with the "AR" class:

"ESTAR ↵ TO BE"	Present Tense	Past Simple	Future
Eu ↵ I	Estou	Estive	Estarei
Tu ↵ You	Estás	Estiveste	Estarás
Ele/Ela ↵ He/She	Está	Esteve	Estará
Nós ↵ We	Estamos	Estivemos	Estaremos
Vós ↵ You	Estais	Estivestes	Estareis
Eles/Elas ↵ They	Estão	Estiveram	Estarão

As for the "ER" group:

"SABER ↬ TO KNOW"	Present Tense	Past Simple	Future
Eu ↬ I	Sei	Soube	Saberei
Tu ↬ You	Sabes	Soubeste	Saberás
Ele/Ela ↬ He/She	Sabe	Soube	Saberá
Nós ↬ We	Sabemos	Soubemos	Saberemos
Vós ↬ You	Sabeis	Soubestes	Sabereis
Eles/Elas ↬ They	Sabem	Souberam	Saberão

Finally, the "IR":

"IR ↶ TO GO"	Present Tense	Past Simple	Future
Eu ↶ I	Vou	Fui	Irei
Tu ↶ You	Vais	Foste	Irás
Ele/Ela ↶ He/She	Vai	Foi	Irá
Nós ↶ We	Vamos	Fomos	Iremos
Vós ↶ You	Ides	Fostes	Ireis
Eles/Elas ↶ They	Vão	Foram	Irão

#2 – Hora de Quiz!

1) Conjugate the verb "ABRAÇAR" in the three tenses we have studied.

2) Conjugate the verb "CORRER" in the three tenses we have studied.

3) Conjugate the verb "SENTIR" in the three tenses we have studied.

4) Conjugate the verb "DAR" in the three tenses we have studied.

5) Conjugate the verb "TER" in the three tenses we have studied.

6) Conjugate the verb "HAVER" in the three tenses we have studied.

7) Conjugate the verb "VIR" in the three tenses we have studied.

8) Rewrite these sentences in the simple past tense:

"Eu adoro aprender Português. Não acho nada difícil."

9) Rewrite these sentences in the future tense:

"Com *Portuguese for Beginners,* eu sei tudo o que é importante. Não há dúvidas."

10) Identify the verbs used in the following sentence, indicating the tenses they are conjugated in:

"Um dia irei a Portugal. Fiz uma promessa, e eu vou cumprir essa promessa.

PART III: CONVERSATION[49]

---

49 The recommended movie for this chapter is "Gaiola Dourada ↪ Golden Cage." It a
French film about Portuguese immigrants and was made by a French director, the son of
Portuguese immigrants. It is very funny and full of simple but realistic dialogue from which
you can learn—while laughing!

Before starting, you should know that, in Portuguese, there is a formal way of communication. This formal way is used in formal situations, with someone you do not know (like a stranger on the street), and as a demonstration of respect for older people. So, instead of using the second-person singular—"TU"—you should use "VOCÊ," conjugating the verb that follows in the third-person singular. However, there is an important thing to remember. The "VOCÊ" is rarely used and is considered rude to insert it into a sentence. So, when speaking formally, whether it is with an older person, an unknown person you just met on the street, or your doctor, the structure of the sentence is the same as it would be with the "VOCÊ" in it, but you either omit it entirely or substitute it for the person's name or equivalent. Like for instance, "O/A SENHOR/A ↪ SIR / MADAM"; "O/A PROFESSOR/A ↪ TEACHER"; "O/A DOUTOR/A ↪ DOCTOR." Look at these examples:

ℵ   "Rita, queres vir comigo ao cinema? ↩ Rita, do you want to come with me to the movies?"

"(A Rita) ~~Você~~ *quer* vir comigo ao cinema?"

ℵ   "Tu és o melhor médico do mundo. ↩ You are the best doctor in the world."

"(O doutor) ~~Você~~ *é* o melhor médico do mundo."

In the following sections, you will see sentences using both forms of communication.

Note: If you are approaching somebody in the street to ask for help, you should use the formal way of communicating, but do not overthink it—the fact that you are making an effort to speak Portuguese to natives will be highly appreciated. No one will see it as disrespectful.

Basic Greetings

- ℵ   Good morning! ↢ Bom dia!

- ℵ   Good evening. ↢ Boa tarde.

- ℵ   Good night. ↢ Boa noite.

- ℵ   Hello/Hi! ↢ Olá!

- ℵ   Welcome to Portugal! ↢ Bem-vindo a Portugal!

- ℵ   How are you[50] feeling today? ↢ Como estás?/ Como te estás a sentir?

- ℵ   We have just arrived! ↢ Acabámos de chegar!

- ℵ   Did you have a nice flight? ↢ Tiveste um bom voo?

- ℵ   Where are you staying at? ↢ Onde é que vão ficar?

- ℵ   Make yourself confortable. ↢ Estás à vontade.

- ℵ   You lost weight! ↢ Perdeste peso!

- ℵ   Long time no see! ↢ Há muito tempo que não te vejo!

- ℵ   I'm excited to see you. ↢ Estou entusiasmado/entusiasmada por ver-te.

- ℵ   Is everything ok? ↢ Está tudo bem?

- ℵ   How are you? ↢ Como estás?

---

[50] Remember that "YOU" can translate to "TU" and "VÓS" (or "VOCÊS"). It depends on how many people the question is being asked to.

א How are you doing? ↵ Como estás?/ Tudo bem?

א You look nice! ↵ Estás com bom aspecto!

א How is your family? ↵ Como está a sua família?

א Where have you been? ↵ Onde tens andado?

א What have you been up to? ↵ O que é que tens feito?

א I didn't see you there, hello! ↵ Não te vi aí, olá!

א I appreciate it. ↵ Eu agradeço, obrigado/a.

א You're welcome! ↵ De nada!

א Nice to meet you. ↵ Prazer em conhecer-te.

א Thank you, bye. ↵ Obrigado/a, adeus, xau.

א Have a nice day. ↵ Tenha um bom dia.

א You too, thanks. ↵ Tu também, obrigada/o.

א Send my regards to X ↵ Manda os meus cumprimentos a X

א See you later! ↵ Até logo!

א See you soon. ↵ Até já.

א Thank you for your help. ↵ Obrigado/a pela ajuda.

א Come back soon. ↵ Volte em breve.

א Come anytime you want/need. ↵ Volta quando quiseres/precisares.

א My condolences. ↵ As minhas condolências, os meus pêsames.

א Give me a kiss! ↵ Dá-me um beijo!

א I'm fine! ↵ Estou bem!

א Let's go! ↵ Vamos!

א Could you translate this for me, please? ↵ Podes traduzir isto para mim, por favor?

א Could you speak more slowly, please? ↵ Podias falar mais devagar, por favor?

א Could you write that down, please? ↵ Podes escrever isso, por favor?

א Do you speak English? ↶ Falas Inglês?

א Excuse me. ↶ Com licença/Desculpe.

א I don't speak portuguese very well. ↶ Eu não falo
Português muito bem.

א I need some help. ↶ Eu preciso de ajuda.

א I only speak English. ↶ Eu só falo Inglês.

א I understand. ↶ Eu percebo/entendo.

Introducing Yourself

א   My name is X. ↶ O meu nome é X., Eu chamo-me X.

א   I live in Albufeira. ↶ Eu vivo em Albufeira.

א   I'm 25 years old. ↶ Eu tenho 25 anos.

א   I have a boyfriend/girlfriend. ↶ Eu tenho namorado/namorada.

א   I'm single. ↶ Estou solteiro/solteira.

א   I'm engaged. ↶ Estou noivo/noiva.

א   I'm married. ↶ Sou casado/casada.

א   My birthday is after tomorrow. ↶ O meu aniversário é depois de amanhã.

א   I work at an office. ↶ Eu trabalho num escritório.

א   I have two pets. ↶ Eu tenho dois animais domésticos.

א   My dream is to be a doctor. ↶ O meu sonho é ser médico.

א   I don't own a car. ↶ Eu não tenho carro.

א   My interests are X. Os meus interesses são X.

Forming Questions and Dialogue

Buying and Ordering

א Can you bring me the menu, please? ↶ Pode trazer-me o menu, por favor?

א Can you help me, please? ↶ Pode ajudar-me, por favor?

א What is today's special? ↶ Qual é o prato do dia?

א I didn't understand, could you repeat, please? ↶ Não percebi, pode repetir, por favor?

א I want to order, please. ↶ Quero fazer o pedido, por favor.

א To drink, I'll have sparkling water. ↶ Para beber quero uma água com gás.

א Where is the bathroom? ↶ Onde é a casa de banho?

א Excuse me, will you let me through? ↶ Desculpe, deixa-me passar?

א I want beef with a side of chips. ↶ Quero um bife com batatas.

א   There is a fly in my soup. ↵ Está uma mosca na minha sopa.

א   The rice is too salty! ↵ O arroz está demasiado salgado.

א   I want to talk with the manager. ↵ Quero falar com o gerente.

א   Do you have takeaway? ↵ Tem comida para levar?

א   Is the order going to take long? ↵ O pedido vai demorar muito?

א   The beef is rare! I want it well done. ↵ O bife está cru! Eu quero-o bem passado.

א   It's delicious! ↵ Está delicioso!

א   What do you recommend? ↵ O que recomenda?

א   What do you have for dessert? ↵ O que tem para sobremesas?

א   Can you bring me the bill, please? ↵ Pode trazer-me a conta, por favor?

א   You can keep the change, thank you. ↵ Pode ficar com o troco, obrigada.

א   Are the vegetables fresh? ↵ Os vegetais são frescos?

א   Where do I find the milk? ↵ Onde posso encontrar o leite?

א   The price is 5,24€. ↵ O preço é 5,24€.[51]

א   Here's 10€. I don't have change, sorry. ↵ Aqui estão 10€. Não tenho trocado, desculpe.

א   That's expensive. Don't you have anything cheaper? ↵ Isso é caro. Não tem nada mais barato?

---

[51] Which is read "cinco euros e vinte e quatro cêntimos ↵ five euros and twenty-four cents."

At Work

‫   The client made a positive review of our service. ↶ O cliente fez um comentário positivo sobre o nosso serviço.

‫   What is the currency in this country? ↶ Qual é a moeda neste país?

‫   It's Euros. Do you know the exchange rate? ↶ É Euros. Sabes qual é a taxa de câmbio?

‫   Can you help me with the customer service? ↶ Podes ajudar-me com o apoio ao cliente?

‫   The boss asked me to do the presentation. ↶ O patrão pediu-me para fazer a apresentação.

‫   The taxes are already included in the price tag. ↶ Os impostos já estão incluídos no preço.

‫   Nice, that makes things easier. Can I pay with VISA card? ↶ Boa, isso torna as coisas mais fáceis. Posso pagar com cartão VISA?

‫   When will we receive the paycheck? ↶ Quando é que vamos receber o salário?

‫   I was about to go do the transfer right now. ↶ Ia fazer a transferência agora mesmo.

‫   So, how can I help you? ↶ Então, como o posso ajudar?

‫   I need to take the day off, I don't feel so good. ↶ Preciso de tirar o dia, não me sinto muito bem.

‫   I need to withdraw money. Where is the ATM[52] machine? ↶ Preciso de levantar dinheiro. Onde é a máquina multibanco?

---

[52] Keep in mind that some ATMs in Portugal might charge a fee for some operations. However, the "multibancos," for most types of cards, won't.

At School/College

✡ Portuguese 101 is going to be in which room? ↻ A aula introdutória de português vai ser em que sala?

✡ We don't have Portuguese 101 today. ↻ Não temos a aula introdutória de Português hoje.

✡ Are we late? ↻ Estamos atrasados?

✡ No, we are early. The teacher always starts 10 minutes after. ↻ Não, estamos adiantados. O/a professor/a começa sempre 10 minutos depois.

✡ May I come in? ↻ Posso entrar?

✡ Yes, have a seat. ↻ Sim, sente-se.

✡ I'm sorry I'm late. ↻ Desculpe o atraso.

✡ Is this seat taken? ↻ Este lugar está ocupado?

✡ No, go ahead. ↻ Não, está à vontade.

✡ Teacher, why is this answer wrong? ↻ Professor, porque é que esta resposta está errada?

✡ Mark, the question was... – Mark, a pergunta era...

✡ I'm going to skip this class, it's so boring. ↻ Vou faltar à aula, é tão aborrecida.

✡ No worries, I'll give you my notes after. ↻ Não te preocupes, eu dou-te os meus apontamentos depois.

✡ May I go to the bathroom? ↻ Posso ir à casa-de-banho?

✡ Teacher, when is the test? ↻ Professor, quando é o teste?

✡ Next Thursday. But you will have the essay about modern art before that! ↻ Na próxima quinta-feira. Mas têm a composição sobre arte moderna antes disso!

✡ Teacher, I didn't understand. Can you explain it again, please? ↻ Professor, não percebi. Pode explicar outra vez, por favor?

ℵ Sure, but pay more attention, X. You are talking a lot. ↵ Claro, mas presta mais atenção, X. Estás a falar muito.

ℵ I have a question: why did the author say that X? ↵ Tenho uma dúvida: porque é que o autor disse que X?

ℵ Can I give my opinion on that matter? ↵ Posso dar a minha opinião sobre esse assunto?

ℵ Did you do the homework? ↵ Fizeste o trabalho de casa?

ℵ I also didn't do it! I was going to ask you the same. ↵ Também não fiz. Ia-te perguntar o mesmo.

ℵ Have you already studied page 22? I don't get it. ↵ Já estudaste a página 22? Não percebo.

ℵ I want you to sit next to me so that I can cheat on the calculus test. ↵ Eu quero que te sentes ao meu lado para poder copiar no teste de cálculo.

ℵ No way. You should have studied. ↵ Nem penses. Devias ter estudado.

ℵ Who is the next group to make the presentation? ↵ Qual é o próximo grupo a apresentar?

ℵ I missed the last lesson. Can you send me an e-mail with the summary? ↵ Faltei à última aula. Podes mandar-me um e-mail com o resumo?

ℵ The teacher didn't show up, I think she's in a conference. ↵ A professora não apareceu. Acho que ela está numa conferência.

ℵ Can you lend me a red pen? ↵ Podes-me emprestar uma caneta vermelha?

ℵ I only have blue markers, sorry. ↵ Só tenho marcadores azuis, desculpa.

ℵ Can you help me with this exercise? ↵ Podes-me ajudar neste exercício?

א   I haven't studied that part yet. ↶ Ainda não estudei essa parte.

א   I'm going to fail in this exam! ↶ Vou chumbar neste exame!

א   Relax, there's still time until the end of the course. ↶ Calma, ainda tens tempo até ao final do curso.

Traveling

א   How much is the ticket? ↶ Quanto custa o bilhete?

א   The flight was turbulent. ↶ O voo foi turbulento.

א   The subway is by the airport. ↶ O metro é perto do aeroporto.

א   Where is the nearest taxi square? ↶ Onde é a praça de táxis mais próxima?

א   I'm going to take the bus. ↶ Vou apanhar o autocarro.

א   At what time does the next train leave? ↶ A que horas é que parte o próximo comboio?

א   Maybe we could rent a car! ↶ Se calhar podemos alugar um carro!

א   Is the hotel within walking distance? ↶ Dá para ir a andar até ao hotel?

א   Don't lose the hotel key. ↶ Não percas a chave do hotel.

א   I'm sharing the room at the hostel. ↶ Estou a partilhar o quarto no hostel.

א   Let's rent a cheap house together! ↶ Vamos arrendar uma casa barata juntos!

א   Bring the map to the sightseeing tour bus. ↶ Traz o mapa para a viagem panorâmica.

א   Can you take me to the nearest hotel? ↶ Pode levar-me ao hotel mais próximo?

א   Here is your key. ↶ Aqui tem a sua chave.

א   I lost my room key. Would you mind giving me another one? ↵ Eu perdi a chave do meu quarto. Importa-se de me dar outra?

א   I'm going to pay in cash. ↵ Vou pagar em dinheiro.

א   Can you get me a receipt? ↵ Pode passar-me factura?

א   I want to write a complaint. ↵ Eu quero escrever uma reclamação.

א   Would you mind calling me a taxi, please? ↵ Importa-se de me chamar um táxi, por favor?

א   What's your destination? ↵ Qual é o seu destino?

א   I need a transfer for the airport. ↵ Preciso de um *transfer* para o aeroporto.

א   Can you take me to this address? ↵ Pode levar-me para esta morada?

א   Two tickets, please. ↵ Dois bilhetes, por favor.

Socializing

א   I missed you! ↵ Tinha saudades tuas!

א   Let's schedule a dinner tomorrow. ↵ Vamos marcar um jantar amanhã.

א   I have a date with him. ↵ Tenho um encontro com ele.

א   Don't you like to party? ↵ Não gostas de festejar?

א   I'll pay the next round! ↵ Eu pago a próxima rodada!

א   Do you come here often? ↵ Vens aqui regularmente?

א   Have you ever been in that restaurant? ↵ Já alguma vez foste aquele restaurante?

א   We saw that movie at the cinema. ↵ Vimos esse filme no cinema.

א   I love to dance! ↵ Adoro dançar!

א   You are the nicest person I ever met. ↵ Tu és a pessoa mais simpática que eu já conheci.

ℵ   I'm in the best mood. ↝ Estou bem disposto!

ℵ   Bring some friends to the party later. ↝ Traz amigos para a festa de logo.

ℵ   Let's have a drink. ↝ Vamos beber um copo.

ℵ   May I join you and your friends? – Posso juntar-me a ti e aos teus amigos?

ℵ   What do you want to drink? ↝ O que quer beber?

ℵ   Do you have any plans for tonight? ↝ Tem alguns planos para hoje?

ℵ   Can I take you to dinner? ↝ Posso levar-te a jantar?

ℵ   Would you like to go get a coffee? ↝ Gostaria de ir tomar um café?

ℵ   I need some help, please. ↝ Eu preciso de ajuda, se faz favor.

ℵ   Can you repeat that, please? ↝ Pode repetir isso, por favor?

ℵ   How do you spell that word? ↝ Como se soletra essa palavra?

ℵ   How do I pronounce it? ↝ Como é que se pronuncia?

Formal Events

ℵ   May I come in? ↝ Posso entrar?

ℵ   Please come in. ↝ Por favor entre.

ℵ   Nice to meet you. ↝ Prazer em conhecê-lo.

ℵ   Likewise. ↝ Igualmente.

ℵ   Please sit over there. ↝ Por favor sente-se ali.

ℵ   Thank you for having me. ↝ Obrigada por me receber.

ℵ   Why did you apply for this job? ↝ Porque se candidatou a este emprego?

ℵ   Because I love the company and what it stands for. ↝ Porque adoro a empresa e aquilo que ela representa.

א	What sparked your interest in this position? ↵ O que suscitou o seu interesse nesta posição?

א	It is what I always wanted to do. ↵ É o que sempre quis fazer.

א	Do you have experience in the area? ↵ Tem experiência na área?

א	Yes, my degree is in X, and I've been working in this business ever since I graduated. ↵ Sim, a minha licenciatura é em X, e tenho trabalhado nesta área desde então.

א	What are your academic credentials? ↵ Quais são as suas credenciais académicas?

א	I have a major in X and a PhD in Y. ↵ Eu tenho uma licenciatura em X, e um doutoramento em Y.

א	What is your *alma mater?* ↵ Qual é a sua Universidade?

א	I studied at X College. ↵ Estudei na Universidade X.

א	What are your biggest strengths? ↵ Quais são os seus pontos fortes?

א	I'm a hard worker, very dynamic, stress resistant, and I'm open to criticism. ↵ Eu sou trabalhador, muito dinâmico, resistente ao stress, e aberto a críticas.

א	What are your weaknesses? ↵ Quais são as suas fraquezas?

א	I'm a perfectionist and very stubborn. ↵ Sou perfecionista e muito teimoso.

א	What are your ambitions regarding this job? ↵ Quais são as suas ambições relativamente a este trabalho?

א	I hope I improve my skills, proving myself of value to the company, and help it grow even more. ↵ Espero melhorar as minhas capacidades, provando ser de valor para a empresa, e ajudando-a a crescer ainda mais.

ℵ   When do you want to start? ↰ Quando quer começar?

ℵ   Now! ↰ Agora!

ℵ   This is the number we had in mind for this specific position. ↰ Este é o valor que tínhamos em mente para esta posição específica.

ℵ   Are you comfortable with it? ↰ Está comfortável com ele?

ℵ   How much were you expecting to earn? ↰ Quanto estava à espera de receber?

ℵ   We liked your interview and application, and will review it carefully. ↰ Gostámos da sua entrevista e candidatura, e vamos revê-la cuidadosamente.

ℵ   Thank you for the opportunity. I will not let you down. ↰ Obrigada pela oportunidadade. Não o desiludirei.

#3 – Hora de Quiz!

1)   Translate the following sentence into Portuguese:

"Hello, ma'am, and good afternoon! My name is João, and I'm 25 years old. I'm visiting Portugal, and I love the weather here. I really want to come back!"

2)   Ask the question that fits the answer:

"Sim, eu gostei muito do nosso jantar de ontem."

3)   How would you ask your teacher to go to the bathroom during the class?

4)   Answer the following questions:

"A que horas irás ao teatro amanhã? Tens um bilhete extra? Posso ir contigo?

5)   Let's say you are unhappy with your salary at the end of the month. Write down a possible conversation you could have with your boss about getting paid what you deserve.

QUIZ ANSWERS

Quiz #1

1)   **Indicate to which class these words belong to:**

א   Carro – common noun;

א   Pessoa – common noun;

א   João – proper noun;

א   Cidade – common noun;

א   Lisboa – proper noun;

א   Pinhal – collective noun;

א   Generosidade – abstract noun;

א   Rapaz – common noun;

א   Aflição – abstract noun;

א   Turma – collective noun;

א   Felicidade – abstract noun;

א   América – proper noun;

א   Alegria – abstract noun;

א   Formigueiro – collective noun;

א   Casal – collective noun;

א   Mondego – proper noun;

- ℵ   Rio - common noun;
- ℵ   Bondade - abstract noun;
- ℵ   Frota - collective noun;
- ℵ   Pensamento - abstract noun.

2)   Highlight the words that can be both proper and common nouns:

- ℵ   **Oliveira** - it can be either the last name of a person, or an olive tree.
- ℵ   **Porto** - It can be the name of a city in Portugal, or a port, a dock.
- ℵ   **Câmara** - It can be the "Câmara Municipal ↝ City Council, or a camera.
- ℵ   **Escola** - it can be the name of a school, that way being a proper noun, or just the place students go to learn, that way being a common noun.

3)   Write the correct definite article—singular or plural, masculine or feminine—before the following words:

- ℵ   **O** carro
- ℵ   **O** sapo
- ℵ   **A** folha
- ℵ   **A** árvore
- ℵ   **Os** corações
- ℵ   **A** televisão
- ℵ   **As** toalhas
- ℵ   **Os** sabonetes

4)   Write the correct indefinite article—singular or plural, masculine or feminine—before the following words:

- ℵ   **Umas** mesas
- ℵ   **Uma** borracha
- ℵ   **Um** afia
- ℵ   **Um** forno

א   **Uns** quadros

א   **Uma** saia

א   **Uma** vela

א   **Um** filme

5)   **Identify the determiners in the sentences, and write down to which group they belong to:**

"**Essa** chave não é **a minha** chave. **Alguém** a roubou! ↶ That key is not my key. Somebody stole it."

"**Cada** um de nós tem **pouco** para fazer. ↶ Each one of us hasn't got much to do."

"**Aquele** animal está **muito** perto de nós. ↶ That animal is very near to us."

"O **vosso** pai é sempre **o mesmo** palerma. ↶ Your dad is always the same dork."

"Eu não sei **quem** tu és. ↶ I don't know who you are."

א   Essa – demonstrative determiner

א   A – definite article

א   Minha – possessive determiner

א   Alguém – indefinite determiner

א   Cada – indefinite determiner

א   Pouco – indefinite determiner

א   Aquele – demonstrative determiner

א   Muito – indefinite determiner

א   Vosso – possessive determiner

א   O – definite article

א   Mesmo – demonstrative determiner

א   Quem – interrogative determiner

6)   **Underline the pronouns in the following sentences:**

"Eu tenho uma bola azul. Vou dá-**la** à Mariana ↶ I have a blue ball. I'm going to give it to Mariana."

"Estás a ver as casas desta rua? **Aquela** é a **minha**. ↪ Are you seeing the houses in this street? That one is my own."

"A Catarina irá cozinhar o jantar. **Ela** cozinha muito bem. ↪ Catarina will cook dinner. She cooks very well."

7) **Insert prepositions to complete the sentences:**

"Eu gosto **de** aprender Português. ↪ I like learning Portuguese."

"O meu avô vai **ao** Hospital. ↪ My grandfather is going to the Hospital."

"O meu cão está **em** casa **do** meu vizinho. ↪ My dog is at my neighbor's house."

8) **Transform the nouns into adjectives and insert them in the following sentences:**

"O meu pai é muito **gordo** (gordura). ↪ My dad is really fat."

"A água está **gelada** (gelo). ↪ The water is freezing."

"Jogar basquetebol é muito **divertido** (diversão). ↪ Playing basketball is really fun."

"Eu acho a escola **aborrecida** (aborrecimento). ↪ I think that school is boring."

9) **Write down these words according to the feminine gender:**

Juíz - juíza; Senhor - senhora; Aluno - aluna; Imperador - imperatriz; Vendedor - vendedora; Actor - actriz; Leitor - leitora; Espanhol - espanhola; Português - portuguesa; Pigmeu - pigmeia; Infante - infanta; Inspector - inspectora; (O) Jornalista - (A) jornalista; Embaixador - embaixadora/embaixatriz; (O) doente - (A) doente.

10) **Write these words in their plural form:**

Mar – mares; Rapaz – rapazes; Pato – patos; Canção – canções; Escrivão – escrivães; Cristão – cristãos; Irmão – irmãos; Alemão –

alemães; Opinião – opiniões; Sótão – sótãos; Paredão – paredões; Farol – faróis; Móvel – móveis; Animal – animais; Funil –funis; Fóssil – fósseis; Nuvem – nuvens; Jardim – jardins.

Quiz #2

1)   Conjugate the verb "ABRAÇAR" in the three tenses we have studied.

"ABRAÇAR ↲ TO HUG"	Present Tense	Past Simple	Future
Eu ↲ I	Abraço	Abraçei	Abraçarei
Tu ↲ You	Abraças	Abraçaste	Abraçarás
Ele/Ela ↲ He/She	Abraça	Abraçou	Abraçará
Nós ↲ We	Abraçamos	Abraçámos	Abraçaremos
Vós ↲ You	Abraçais	Abraçastes	Abraçareis
Eles/Elas ↲ They	Abraçam	Abraçaram	Abraçarão

2)   Conjugate the verb "CORRER" in the three tenses we have studied.

"CORRER ↲ CAN"	Present Tense	Past Simple	Future
Eu ↲ I	Corro	Corri	Correrei
Tu ↲ You	Corres	Correste	Correrás
Ele/Ela ↲ He/She	Corre	Correu	Correrá
Nós ↲ We	Corremos	Corremos	Correremos
Vós ↲ You	Correis	Correstes	Correreis
Eles/Elas ↲ They	Correm	Correram	Correrão

3)   Conjugate the verb "SENTIR" in the three tenses we have studied.

"SENTIR ↻ TO FEEL"	Present Tense	Past Simple	Future
Eu ↻ I	Sinto	Senti	Sentirei
Tu ↻ You	Sentes	Sentiste	Sentirás
Ele/Ela ↻ He/She	Sente	Sentiu	Sentirá
Nós ↻ We	Sentimos	Sentimos	Sentiremos
Vós ↻ You	Sentis	Sentistes	Sentireis
Eles/Elas ↻ They	Sentem	Sentiram	Sentirão

4) Conjugate the verb "DAR" in the three tenses we have studied.

"DAR ↻ TO GIVE"	Present Tense	Past Simple	Future
Eu ↻ I	Dou	Dei	Darei
Tu ↻ You	Dás	Deste	Darás
Ele/Ela ↻ He/She	Dá	Deu	Dará
Nós ↻ We	Damos	Demos	Daremos
Vós ↻ You	Dais	Destes	Dareis
Eles/Elas ↻ They	Dão	Deram	Darão

5) Conjugate the verb "TER" in the three tenses we have studied.

"TER ↻ TO	Present	Past Simple	Future

HAVE"	Tense		
Eu ↵ I	Tenho	Tive	Terei
Tu ↵ You	Tens	Tiveste	Terás
Ele/Ela ↵ He/She	Tem	Teve	Terá
Nós ↵ We	Temos	Tivemos	Teremos
Vós ↵ You	Tendes	Tivestes	Tereis
Eles/Elas ↵ They	Têm	Tiveram	Terão

6)   Conjugate the verb "HAVER" in the three tenses we have studied.

"HAVER ↵ TO EXIST, or TO HAVE"	Present Tense	Past Simple	Future
Eu ↵ I	Hei	Houve	Haverei
Tu ↵ You	Hás	Houveste	Haverás
Ele/Ela ↵ He/She	Há	Houve	Haverá
Nós ↵ We	Havemos	Houvemos	Haveremos
Vós ↵ You	Haveis	Houvestes	Havereis
Eles/Elas ↵ They	Hão	Houveram	Haverão

7)   Conjugate the verb "VIR" in the three tenses we have studied.

"VIR ↵ TO	Present Tense	Past Simple	Future

COME"			
Eu ↪ I	Vou	Vim	Virei
Tu ↪ You	Vais	Vieste	Virás
Ele/Ela ↪ He/She	Vai	Veio	Virá
Nós ↪ We	Vamos	Viémos	Viremos
Vós ↪ You	Vindes	Viestes	Vireis
Eles/Elas ↪ They	Vão	Vieram	Virão

8)   Rewrite these sentences in the simple past tense:

"Eu adoro aprender Português. Não acho nada difícil."

We are facing two regular verbs—"ADORAR" and "ACHAR"—so in the past simple, they follow the rules we learned:

"Eu **adorei** aprender Português. Não **achei** nada difícil."

9)   Rewrite these sentences in the future tense:

"Com *Portuguese for Beginners,* eu sei tudo o que é importante. Não tenho mais dúvidas."

The verb "SABER" is irregular. However, as you probably noticed, in the future indicative, hardly anything changes among the three groups of verb endings. The same applies to the irregular verb "TO HAVE."

"Com *Portuguese for Beginners,* eu **saberei** tudo o que é importante. Não **terei** mais dúvidas.

10)   Identify the verbs used in the following sentence, indicating the tenses they are conjugated in:

"Um dia irei a Portugal. Fiz uma promessa, e eu vou cumprir essa promessa."

"IREI" - verb "IR ↝ TO GO" - future indicative tense

"FIZ" - verb "FAZER ↝ TO DO" - past simple tense

"VOU" - "IR ↝ TO GO" - presente tense

"CUMPRIR" - "CUMPRIR ↝ TO ACCOMPLISH (but in this case, the verb "CUMPRIR" means to maintain, or keep the promise) - in the infinitive.

Quiz #3[53]

1)   Translate into Portuguese the following sentence:

"Hello, ma'am, and good afternoon! My name is João, and I'm twenty-five years old. I'm visiting Portugal, and I love the weather here. I really want to come back!"

"Olá (minha)[54] senhora, e boa tarde! O meu nome é João, e tenho vinte e cinco anos. Estou a visitor Portugal e adoro o tempo aqui. Eu quero mesmo voltar!"

2)   Ask the question that fits the answer:

"Eu gostei muito do nosso jantar de ontem."

"Tu gostaste do nosso jantar ontem? ↝ Did you like our dinner yesterday?"

---

53 Since this quiz demands a few open answers, the proposed solutions are merely indications of what the right answer should look like. Variations of the sentences presented, and other answers, might work as well. The answers shown just provide an orientation—one solution with several other possibilities. Be creative!

54 The word "minha" is not essential to the translation; however, it is considered indelicate if not used when talking to an older woman, just using instead "senhora" by itself. Even though it doesn't mean the same, it can compare to the expression "my dear sir"—simply put, it is just nicer to say it like that.

"O que achaste do nosso jantar ontem? ↳ What did you think of our dinner yesterday?"

3)   How would you ask your teacher to go to the bathroom during the class?

"Professor/a, posso ir à casa de banho, se faz favor? ↳ Teacher/Professor, may I go to the bathroom, please?"

4)   Answer the following questions:

"A que horas irás ao teatro amanhã? Tens um bilhete extra? Posso ir contigo? ↳ "At what time will you go to the theatre tomorrow? Do you have an extra ticket? Can I go with you?

"Amanhã vou ao teatro às X horas. Sim, tenho um bilhete extra./ Não, não tenho um bilhete extra. Sim, podes ir comigo./ Não, não podes ir comigo. ↳ Tomorrow I will go to the theatre at X o'clock. Yes, I have an extra ticket/No, I don't have an extra ticket. Yes, you can go with me/ No, you can't go with me."

5)   Let's say you're unhappy with your salary at the end of the month. Write down a possible conversation you could have with your boss about finally getting paid what you deserve.[55]

- Bom dia[56], Chefe[57], posso entrar? ↳ Good morning, Boss, may I come in?

- Sim, claro que sim. ↳ Yes, of course.

- Como está, Chefe? ↳ How are you, Boss?

- Comigo está tudo bem. E consigo? Porque decidiu falar comigo hoje? or O que quer? or Qual é o assunto/problema? ↳ Everything is

---

fine with me. What about you? Why did you decide to speak to me today? or What do you want? or What is the matter/problem?

- Comigo também está tudo bem, obrigado.[58] Chefe, estou aqui para falar consigo porque quero discutir o meu salário, or Eu acho que recebo menos do que devia, or Eu penso que o meu salário é baixo, or Eu queria ganhar mais dinheiro. ↵ I'm fine as well, thank you. Boss, I am here to talk to you because I want to discuss my salary, or I think I get less than I deserve, or I think that my salary is low, or I want to make more money.

- Porque diz isso? or Porque pensa assim? ↵ Why do you say that? or Why do you think that?

- Penso assim porque trabalho muito e creio que mereço um aumento. Já trabalho na empresa há X anos. ↵ I think this way because I work a lot and I think I deserve a raise. I have been working for this company for X years.

- Muito bem. O que propõe? ↵ Very well. What do you propose?

- Bem, eu proponho um aumento de X euros. ↵ Well, I propose a raise of X euros.

- Você é um bom trabalhador e é verdade que merece um aumento. Dito isto, vou pensar no valor que propôs. ↵ You are a good worker and it is true that you deserve a raise. With this being said, I am going to think about the amount you proposed.

- Obrigado, Chefe. ↵ Thank you, Boss.

- De nada. ↵ You are welcome.[59]

---

58 Or "obrigad*A*" if you are a woman.

59 Yes—if only asking for a raise would be that easy... We can dream, though!

APPENDIX: VOCABULARY

It is impossible to compile all of the words that you need to learn in one section, or even in one book. Nevertheless, this guide has provided you with, at the very least, the most important vocabulary, which is used frequently, and that you will definitely use or hear when traveling to a Portuguese-speaking country, watching a Portuguese movie, or listening to Portuguese music.

On the following pages, you will find lists of vocabularies that contain some words which were **not** used in the previous chapters. So, if you find that some indispensable word is not within these lists, search for it in a section that might be related to it[60]. Even if you have to reread the book, that won't be time wasted! Aside from the words that are considered fundamental, this guide has also added some that might be used less often, but that will enrich your vocabulary, granting you the opportunity to brag and "flex" in front of your friends and family.

---

60 For instance, the days of the week, months, or seasons of the year are in PART I: THE VERY BASICS.

Glossary of Nouns

Animals

א   Anchovy ↝ Anchova

א   Ant ↝ Formiga

א   Bear ↝ Urso

א   Bee ↝ Abelha

א   Bird ↝ Pássaro

א   Bug ↝ Bicho / Insecto

א   Bull ↝ Touro

א   Butterfly ↝ Borboleta

א   Cat ↝ Gato

א   Chicken↝ Galinha/Frango

א   Clams ↝ Amêijoas

א   Cock/Rooster ↝ Galo

א   Codfish ↝ Bacalhau

א   Cow ↝ Vaca

א   Crab ↝ Caranguejo

א   Crow ↝ Corvo

א   Deer ↝ Veado

א   Dog ↝ Cão

ℵ   Dove ↶ Pomba

ℵ   Dragon ↶ Dragão

ℵ   Duck ↶ Pato

ℵ   Eagle ↶ Águia

ℵ   Elephant ↶ Elefante

ℵ   Fish ↶ Peixe

ℵ   Flies ↶ Moscas

ℵ   Fly ↶ Mosca

ℵ   Fox ↶ Raposa

ℵ   Frog ↶ Sapo

ℵ   Giraffe ↶ Girafa

ℵ   Goat ↶ Cabra

ℵ   Gorilla ↶ Gorila

ℵ   Hake ↶ Pescada

ℵ   Hippopotamus ↶ Hipópotamo

ℵ   Hoof ↶ Casco

ℵ   Horse mackerel ↶ Carapau

ℵ   Horse ↶ Cavalo

ℵ   Insect ↶ Insecto

ℵ   Lamb ↶ Cordeiro

ℵ   Leopard ↶ Leopardo

ℵ   Lion ↶ Leão

ℵ   Monkey ↶ Macaco

ℵ   Mosquitoes ↶ Mosquitos

ℵ   Mouse ↶ Rato

ℵ   Owl ↶ Coruja

ℵ   Parrot ↶ Papagaio

ℵ   Paw ↶ Pata

ℵ   Pig ↶ Porco

ℵ   Pigeon ↶ Pombo

ℵ   Pork ↶ Porco

- ℵ Rabbit ↝ Coelho
- ℵ Rat ↝ Ratazana
- ℵ Rattlesnake ↝ Cascavel
- ℵ Razor Clam ↝ Lingueirão
- ℵ Salmon ↝ Salmão
- ℵ Sardine ↝ Sardinha
- ℵ Sea Bass ↝ Robalo
- ℵ Sea Bream ↝ Dourada
- ℵ Seahorse ↝ Cavalo-marinho
- ℵ Serpent ↝ Serpente
- ℵ Shark ↝ Tubarão
- ℵ Sheep ↝ Ovelha
- ℵ Shellfish ↝ Marisco
- ℵ Snake ↝ Cobra
- ℵ Spider ↝ Aranha
- ℵ Tail ↝ Cauda
- ℵ Tiger ↝ Tigre
- ℵ Trout ↝ Truta
- ℵ Trunk (Elephant's) ↝ Tromba
- ℵ Tuna ↝ Atum
- ℵ Turkey ↝ Peru
- ℵ Wasp ↝ Vespa
- ℵ Whelk ↝ Búzios
- ℵ Wing ↝ Asa
- ℵ Wolf ↝ Lobo

Body and Health

- ℵ Achilles' Tendon ↝ Tendão de Aquiles
- ℵ Adam's Apple ↝ Maçã-de-Adão
- ℵ Anatomy ↝ Anatomia
- ℵ Ankle ↝ Tornozelo

- Anus ↝ Ânus
- Appendix ↝ Apêndice
- Arm ↝ Braço
- Armpit ↝ Axila/Sovaco
- Artery ↝ Artéria
- Back ↝ Costas
- Backbone ↝ Coluna vertebral
- Beard ↝ Barba
- Belly button ↝ Umbigo
- Belly ↝ Barriga
- Big toe ↝ Dedo grande
- Bile ↝ Bílis
- Bladder ↝ Bexiga
- Blood ↝ Sangue
- Bone ↝ Osso
- Bottom ↝ Rabo
- Boy ↝ Rapaz/Menino
- Brain ↝ Cérebro
- Breasts ↝ Seios
- Breath ↝ Hálito
- Buttocks ↝ Nádegas
- Calf (body part) ↝ Gémeo
- Cartilage ↝ Cartilagem
- Cheek ↝ Bochecha
- Chest ↝ Peito
- Child ↝ Criança
- Chin ↝ Queixo
- Collarbone ↝ Clavícula
- Cornea ↝ Córnea
- Ear ↝ Orelha/Ouvido
- Eardrum ↝ Tímpano

- Earlobe ↩ Lóbulo da orelha
- Elbow ↩ Cotovelo
- Eye ↩ Olho
- Eyeball ↩ Globo ocular
- Eyebrow ↩ Sobrancelha
- Eyelash ↩ Pestana
- Eyelid ↩ Pálpebra
- Fat ↩ Gordura
- Finger ↩ Dedos
- Fingernail ↩ Unha
- Foot ↩ Pé
- Forearm ↩ Antebraço
- Forehead ↩ Testa
- Freckles ↩ Sardas
- Fur ↩ Pêlo
- Gland ↩ Glândula
- Groin ↩ Virilha
- Hair ↩ Cabelo
- Hand ↩ Mão
- Head ↩ Cabeça
- Hearing/sound ↩ Audição
- Heart ↩ Coração
- Heel ↩ Calcanhar
- Hiccup ↩ Soluço
- Hip ↩ Anca
- Intestines ↩ Intestino
- Iris ↩ Íris
- Jaw ↩ Maxilar
- Joints ↩ Articulações
- Kidneys ↩ Rins
- Knee ↩ Joelho

- א   Kneecap ↝ Rótula
- א   Knuckles ↝ Nós dos dedos
- א   Large intestine ↝ Intestino grosso
- א   Leg ↝ Perna
- א   Limb ↝ Membro
- א   Lip ↝ Lábio
- א   Liver ↝ Fígado
- א   Lungs ↝ Pulmões
- א   Man ↝ Homem
- א   Menstruation ↝ Menstruação
- א   Mustache ↝ Bigode
- א   Mouth ↝ Boca
- א   Mucus ↝ Muco
- א   Muscle ↝ Músculo
- א   Neck ↝ Pescoço
- א   Nerve ↝ Nervo
- א   Nervous System ↝ Sistema nervoso
- א   Nipple ↝ Mamilo
- א   Nose ↝ Nariz
- א   Nostril ↝ Narina
- א   Esophagus ↝ Esófago
- א   Organ ↝ Orgão
- א   Palm ↝ Palma
- א   Pancreas ↝ Pâncreas
- א   Pelvis ↝ Pélvis
- א   Period ↝ Período
- א   Pregnant ↝ Grávida
- א   Pupil ↝ Pupila
- א   Rectum ↝ Recto
- א   Retina ↝ Retina
- א   Rib cage ↝ Caixa Torácica

א   Rib ~ Costela

א   Saliva/spit ~ Saliva/cuspe

א   Semen ~ Sémen

א   Senses ~ Sentidos

א   Shin ~ Canela

א   Sick ~ Doente, enjoado

א   Shoulder ~ Ombro

א   Skeleton ~ Esqueleto

א   Skin ~ Pele

א   Skull ~ Crânio

א   Small Intestine ~ Intestino delgado

א   Smell ~ Olfacto

א   Sneeze ~ Espirro

א   Sole ~ Planta (do pé)

א   Spleen ~ Baço

א   Stomach ~ Estômago

א   Sweat ~ Suor

א   Taste ~ Palato/paladar

א   Tears ~ Lágrimas

א   Teeth ~ Dentes

א   Tendon ~ Tendão

א   Testicles ~ Testículos

א   Thigh bone/femur ~ Fémur

א   Thigh ~ Coxa

א   Throat ~ Garganta

א   Thumb ~ Polegar

א   Tingling ~ Formigueiro[61]

א   Toe ~ Dedo do pé

א   Toenail ~ Unha do pé

---

61 "Formigueiro" is also the word for "anthill," and an ant is a "formiga."

- ℵ   Tongue ⤳ Língua
- ℵ   Tooth ⤳ Dente
- ℵ   Touch ⤳ Tacto
- ℵ   Urine ⤳ Urina
- ℵ   Vagina ⤳ Vagina
- ℵ   Vein ⤳ Veia
- ℵ   Vertebra ⤳ Vértebra
- ℵ   Vomit ⤳ Vómito
- ℵ   Waist ⤳ Cintura
- ℵ   Windpipe ⤳ Traqueia
- ℵ   Woman ⤳ Mulher
- ℵ   Womb ⤳ Útero
- ℵ   Wrinkles ⤳ Rugas
- ℵ   Wrist ⤳ Pulso

Cardinal Points

- ℵ   N ⤳ N
- ℵ   S ⤳ S
- ℵ   W ⤳ O
- ℵ   E ⤳ E/L
- ℵ   NE ⤳ NE
- ℵ   NW ⤳ NO
- ℵ   SE ⤳ SE
- ℵ   SW ⤳ SO
- ℵ   North ⤳ Norte
- ℵ   South ⤳ Sul
- ℵ   West ⤳ Oeste/Ocidente/Poente
- ℵ   East ⤳ Este/Leste/Oriente/Nascente/Levante
- ℵ   Northeast ⤳ Nordeste
- ℵ   Northwest ⤳ Noroeste
- ℵ   Southeast ⤳ Sudeste

א Southwest ↵ Sudoeste

Clothes

א Blouse ↵ Blusa

א Bra(ssiere) ↵ Soutien

א Dress ↵ Vestido

א Fashion ↵ Moda

א Gloves ↵ Luvas

א Hat ↵ Chapéu

א High heels ↵ Sapatos de salto alto

א Jacket ↵ Casaco

א Pants ↵ Calças

א Shoes ↵ Sapatos / Calçado

א Shorts ↵ Calções

א Skirt ↵ Saia

א Sneakers ↵ Sapatilhas / Ténis

א Socks ↵ Meias

א Suit ↵ Fato

א Swimsuit ↵ Fato de banho

א (Under) panties ↵ Cuecas

א Underwear ↵ Roupa interior

Colors

א Black ↵ Preto

א Blue ↵ Azul

א Brown ↵ Castanho

א Gray ↵ Cinzento

א Green ↵ Verde

א Orange ↵ Cor-de-laranja

א Pink ↵ Cor-de-rosa

א Purple ↵ Roxo

ℵ   Red ↪ Vermelho

ℵ   Turquoise ↪ Turquesa

ℵ   White ↪ Branco

ℵ   Yellow ↪ Amarelo

Family

ℵ   Aunt ↪ Tia

ℵ   Baby ↪ Bebé

ℵ   Best friend ↪ Melhor amigo/a

ℵ   Boyfriend ↪ Namorado

ℵ   Brother ↪ Irmão

ℵ   Brother-in-law ↪ Cunhado

ℵ   Couple ↪ Casal

ℵ   Cousin ↪ Primo/a

ℵ   Daughter ↪ Filha

ℵ   Daughter-in-law ↪ Nora

ℵ   Family ↪ Família

ℵ   Father-in-law ↪ Sogro

ℵ   Fiancé ↪ Noivo

ℵ   Fiancée ↪ Noiva

ℵ   Friend ↪ Amigo/a

ℵ   Gentleman ↪ Cavalheiro

ℵ   Girl ↪ Rapariga/Menina

ℵ   Girlfriend ↪ Namorada

ℵ   Goddaughter ↪ Afilhada

ℵ   Godfather ↪ Padrinho

ℵ   Godmother ↪ Madrinha

ℵ   Godson ↪ Aflhado

ℵ   Granddaughter ↪ Neta

ℵ   Grandfather ↪ Avô

ℵ   Grandmother ↪ Avó

א Grandparents ⤻ Avós
א Grandson ⤻ Neto
א Husband ⤻ Marido
א Ma'am ⤻ (Minha) Senhora
א Mother-in-law ⤻ Sogra
א Mr. ⤻ Senhor
א Mrs. ⤻ Senhora
א Nephew ⤻ Sobrinho
א Niece ⤻ Sobrinha
א Sir ⤻ Senhor
א Sister ⤻ Irmã
א Sister-in-law ⤻ Cunhada
א Son ⤻ Filho
א Son-in-law ⤻ Genro
א Stepdaughter ⤻ Enteada
א Stepfather ⤻ Padrasto
א Stepmother ⤻ Madrasta
א Stepson ⤻ Enteado
א Uncle ⤻ Tio
א Wife ⤻ Esposa

Food, Drinks and Eating

א Apple ⤻ Maçã
א Banana ⤻ Banana
א Barley ⤻ Cevada
א Beef ⤻ Vaca
א Beer ⤻ Cerveja
א Beverages ⤻ Bebidas
א Bread counter ⤻ Padaria
א Butter ⤻ Manteiga
א Cereal ⤻ Cereais

- א   Cheese ↜ Queijo
- א   Cherry ↜ Cereja
- א   Chocolate ↜ Chocolate
- א   Cider ↜ Sidra[62]
- א   Coconut ↜ Coco
- א   Coffee ↜ Café
- א   Corn ↜ Milho
- א   Cutlery ↜ Talheres
- א   Desserts ↜ Sobremesas
- א   Drinks ↜ Bebidas
- א   Egg ↜ Ovo
- א   Flesh ↜ Carne
- א   Food ↜ Comida
- א   Freezing ↜ Gelado
- א   Full ↜ Cheio/a
- א   Garlic ↜ Alho
- א   Grapes ↜ Uvas
- א   Ham ↜ Fiambre
- א   Ice cream ↜ Gelado
- א   Jam ↜ Compota
- א   Juice ↜ Sumo
- א   Lemon ↜ Limão
- א   Lemonade ↜ Limonada
- א   Lime ↜ Lima
- א   Meat section ↜ Talho
- א   Meat ↜ Carne
- א   Milk ↜ Leite
- א   Milkshake ↜ Batido

---

[62] Note that the very similar word "CIDRA" doesn't mean the same thing, but instead it ‚means "CITRON".

- א Mushroom ∽ Cogumelo
- א Nuts ∽ Frutos Secos
- א Oat ∽ Aveia
- א Olive Oil ∽ Azeite
- א Olives ∽ Azeitonas
- א Onion ∽ Cebola
- א Orange ∽ Laranja
- א Peanut Butter ∽ Manteiga de Amendoim
- א Peanuts ∽ Amendoins
- א Pear ∽ Pêra
- א Pepper ∽ Pimenta
- א Pineapple ∽ Ananás
- א Salt ∽ Sal
- א Sangria ∽ Sangria
- א Sausage ∽ Salsicha
- א Soda ∽ Refrigerante
- א Sour ∽ Azedo
- א Spicy ∽ Picante
- א Spine ∽ Espinha
- א Strawberries ∽ Morangos
- א Sweet ∽ Doce
- א Tea ∽ Chá
- א Vegetables ∽ Vegetais
- א Vinegar ∽ Vinagre
- א Vitamin Pills ∽ Vitamínicos
- א Water ∽ Água
- א Wheat ∽ Trigo
- א Wine ∽ Vinho

Household Items

- א Baby food ∽ Comida de bebé

- ℵ   Baby wipes ↝ Toalhitas de bebé
- ℵ   Backpack ↝ Mochila
- ℵ   Bag ↝ Saco
- ℵ   Batteries ↝ Pilhas
- ℵ   Books ↝ Livros
- ℵ   Bottle ↝ Garrafa
- ℵ   Bowl ↝ Tigela
- ℵ   Candle ↝ Vela
- ℵ   Card ↝ Cartão
- ℵ   Clock ↝ Relógio
- ℵ   Cologne ↝ Colónia
- ℵ   Conditioner ↝ Amaciador
- ℵ   Condoms ↝ Preservativos
- ℵ   Cotton ↝ Algodão
- ℵ   Cup ↝ Chávena
- ℵ   Cutlery - Talheres
- ℵ   Dental floss ↝ Fio dental
- ℵ   Deodorant ↝ Desodorizante
- ℵ   Diapers ↝ Fraldas
- ℵ   Door lock ↝ Fechadura da porta
- ℵ   Envelopes ↝ Envelopes
- ℵ   Face powder ↝ Pó de arroz
- ℵ   Firewood ↝ Lenha
- ℵ   First aid kit ↝ Kit de Primeiros Socorros
- ℵ   Flashlight ↝ Lanterna
- ℵ   Fork ↝ Garfo
- ℵ   Foundation ↝ Base
- ℵ   Funnel ↝ Funil
- ℵ   Furniture ↝ Móveis
- ℵ   Glass (as in the "glass of a window") ↝ Vidro
- ℵ   Glass (as in a "glass of water") ↝ Copo

- Glue ↝ Cola
- Hairbrush ↝ Escova do cabelo
- Hairspray ↝ Laca
- Handkerchiefs ↝ Lenços
- Headphones ↝ Auscultadores
- Ice ↝ Gelo
- Jelly ↝ Gelatina
- Knife ↝ Faca
- Lamp ↝ Lamparina
- Laxatives ↝ Laxantes
- Light bulb ↝ Lâmpada
- Lighter ↝ Isqueiro
- Lipstick ↝ Baton
- Locker ↝ Cadeado
- Magazines ↝ Revistas
- Mascara ↝ Rímel
- Matches ↝ Fósforos
- Mirror ↝ Espelho
- Moisturizing cream ↝ Creme hidratante
- Mouthwash ↝ Elixir Bocal
- Nail scissors ↝ Corta-unhas
- Napkin ↝ Guardanapo
- Needle ↝ Agulha
- Newspaper ↝ Jornal
- Oil ↝ Óleo
- Ointment ↝ Pomada
- Painkillers ↝ Analgésicos
- Paper ↝ Papel
- Pen ↝ Caneta
- Pencil ↝ Lápis
- Perfume ↝ Perfume

- Phone charger ↭ Carregador de Telemóvel
- Photographs ↭ Fotografias
- Plate ↭ Prato
- Pot ↭ Panela
- Razor ↭ Lâmina/gillette
- Rope ↭ Corda
- Sanitary pad ↭ Penso higiénico
- Sanitary towels ↭ Toalhitas higiénicas
- Scarf ↭ Lenço
- Scissors ↭ Tesouras
- Serum ↭ Soro
- Shampoo ↭ Champô
- Shaving cream ↭ Creme de barbear
- Shaving foam ↭ Espuma de barbear
- Shaving gel ↭ Gel de barbear
- Sleeping bag ↭ Saco-cama
- Soap ↭ Sabão
- Sofa ↭ Sofá
- Souvenirs ↭ Lembranças
- Spoon ↭ Colher
- Straws ↭ Palhinhas
- Sun lotion ↭ Protector solar
- Sunglasses ↭ Óculos de Sol
- Tablecloth ↭ Toalha de mesa
- Tampons ↭ Tampões
- Telephone ↭ Telefone
- Television ↭ Televisão
- Tent ↭ Tenda
- Thermometer ↭ Termómetro
- Tissues ↭ Lenços
- Toilet paper ↭ Papel higiénico

- א Toothbrush ↝ Escova de dentes
- א Toothpaste ↝ Pasta de dentes
- א Tweezers ↝ Pinças
- א Umbrella ↝ Chapéu de chuva
- א Utensils ↝ Utensílios
- א Valve ↝ Válvula
- א Watch ↝ Relógio
- א Wristwatch ↝ Relógio de pulso

Instruments[63]

- א Accordion ↝ Acordeão
- א Bagpipe ↝ Gaita-de-foles
- א Bass ↝ Baixo
- א Drums ↝ Bateria
- א Cello ↝ Violencelo
- א Clarinet ↝ Clarinete
- א Classical guitar ↝ Guitarra clássica
- א Flute ↝ Flauta
- א Guitar ↝ Guitarra
- א Guitarrist (or Guitar Player) ↝ Guitarrista
- א Harp ↝ Harpa
- א Piano ↝ Piano
- א Saxophone ↝ Saxofone
- א Tambourine ↝ Pandeireta
- א Triangle ↝ Triângulo
- א Viola ↝ Violão
- א Violin ↝ Violino

---

63 There are two very famous Portuguese instruments. They are called the "cavaquinho," which is a small guitar, cousin of the ukulele, and the "guitarra Portuguesa," which literally means "Portuguese guitar" and is used mainly to go along with Fado. Just search for it on YouTube, and you will find some tunes that will give you goosebumps!

א   Xylophone ↪ Xilofone

Means of Transportation

א   Accelerator ↪ Acelerador

א   Accident ↪ Acidente

א   Airport ↪ Aeroporto

א   Automatic ↪ Automático

א   Avenue ↪ Avenida

א   Back seat ↪ Lugar de trás

א   Battery ↪ Bateria

א   Beam ↪ Faról

א   Belt ↪ Cinto

א   Bicycle ↪ Bicicleta

א   Blinkers ↪ Piscas

א   Boat ↪ Barco

א   Brake light ↪ Luz de travagem

א   Bumper ↪ Pára-choques

א   Cable ↪ Cabo

א   Car ↪ Carro

א   Caravan ↪ Caravana

א   Child seat ↪ Cadeira de criança

א   Clutch ↪ Embraiagem

א   Convertible ↪ Descapotável

א   Cyclist ↪ Ciclista

א   Dashboard ↪ Tablier

א   Diesel ↪ Gasóleo

א   Driver's seat ↪ Lugar do condutor

א   Exhaust ↪ Exaustor

א   Flat tire ↪ Pneu furado

א   Front seat ↪ Lugar da frente

א   Fuel tank ↪ Depósito de combustível

- ℵ Fuel ↩ Combustível
- ℵ Full beam lights ↩ Máximos
- ℵ Fuse ↩ Fusível
- ℵ Garage ↩ Garage
- ℵ Gas pedal ↩ Acelerador
- ℵ Gas ↩ Gás
- ℵ Gasoline ↩ Gasolina
- ℵ Glove compartment ↩ Porta-luvas
- ℵ Handbrake ↩ Travão
- ℵ Headlights ↩ Faróis
- ℵ Headrest ↩ Encosto
- ℵ Helicopter ↩ Helicóptero
- ℵ Horn ↩ Buzina
- ℵ Ignition ↩ Ignição
- ℵ Indicators ↩ Indicadores
- ℵ Insurance ↩ Seguro
- ℵ Jack ↩ Macaco do carro
- ℵ Kite ↩ Pipa
- ℵ Leather ↩ Couro
- ℵ Left ↩ Esquerda
- ℵ Mechanic ↩ Mecânico
- ℵ Minibus ↩ Miniautocarro
- ℵ Motor ↩ Motor
- ℵ Motorbike ↩ Motocicleta
- ℵ Number (or Licence) plate ↩ Matrícula
- ℵ Passenger seat ↩ Lugar do passageiro/pendura
- ℵ Piston ↩ Pistão
- ℵ Pressure ↩ Pressão
- ℵ Radiator ↩ Radiador
- ℵ Rear windscreen ↩ Pára-brisas traseiro
- ℵ Rearview mirror ↩ Espelho retrovisor

א   Right ↵ Left

א   Road ↵ Estrada

א   Roof ↵ Tecto

א   Scooter ↵ Scooter

א   Seatbelt ↵ Cinto de segurança

א   Shock absorber ↵ Pára-choques

א   Snow tires ↵ Pneus para a neve

א   Spare tire ↵ Pneu sobresselente

א   Speedometer ↵ Velocímetro

א   Steering wheel ↵ Volante

א   Taxi ↵ Táxi

א   Tire ↵ Pneu

א   Tractor ↵ Tractor

א   Trailer ↵ Atrelado

א   Tram ↵ Elétrico

א   Truck ↵ Camião

א   Trunk (of the car) ↵ Bagageira

א   Unleaded gas ↵ Gasolina sem chumbo

א   Van ↵ Carrinha

א   Warning light ↵ Luz de aviso

א   Window ↵ Janela

א   Windscreen ↵ Pára-brisas

Nature

א   Apple tree ↵ Macieira

א   Branch ↵ Ramo

א   Breeze ↵ Brisa

א   Bush ↵ Arbusto

א   Cactus ↵ Cacto

א   Cherry tree ↵ Cerejeira

א   Chestnut tree ↵ Castanheiro

- א   Climate ↪ Clima
- א   Cloud ↪ Nuvem
- א   Clouds ↪ Nuvens
- א   Cold ↪ Frio
- א   Drought ↪ Seca
- א   Dry ↪ Seco
- א   Fig tree ↪ Figueira
- א   Fire ↪ Fogo
- א   Flower ↪ Flor
- א   Fog ↪ Nevoeiro
- א   Fossil ↪ Fóssil
- א   Fruit tree ↪ Árvore de fruto
- א   Fruits ↪ Frutas
- א   Garden ↪ Jardim
- א   Grass ↪ Relva
- א   Heat ↪ Calor
- א   Herb ↪ Erva
- א   Hot ↪ Quente
- א   Humidity ↪ Humidade
- א   Hurricane ↪ Furacão
- א   Leaf ↪ Folha
- א   Lightning ↪ Trovão
- א   Meteorology ↪ Metereologia
- א   Moon ↪ Lua
- א   Moonlight ↪ Luar
- א   Moss ↪ Musgo
- א   Mountains ↪ Montanhas
- א   Olive tree ↪ Oliveira
- א   Outdoor ↪ Exterior
- א   Palm tree ↪ Palmeira
- א   Pear tree ↪ Pereira

- ℵ   Petal ↝ Pétala
- ℵ   Pine forest ↝ Pinhal
- ℵ   Pine tree ↝ Pinheiro
- ℵ   Plants ↝ Plantas
- ℵ   Plum tree ↝ Pessegueiro
- ℵ   Pollen ↝ Pólen
- ℵ   Rain ↝ Chuva
- ℵ   Rainbow ↝ Arco-íris
- ℵ   Region ↝ Região
- ℵ   River ↝ Rio
- ℵ   Root ↝ Raiz
- ℵ   Rose ↝ Rosa
- ℵ   Sea ↝ Mar
- ℵ   Sky ↝ Céu
- ℵ   Snow ↝ Neve
- ℵ   Storm ↝ Tempestade
- ℵ   Sunny ↝ Soalheiro (or solarengo)
- ℵ   Temperature ↝ Temperatura
- ℵ   Thorn ↝ Espinho
- ℵ   Thunder ↝ Trovoada
- ℵ   Tornado ↝ Tornado
- ℵ   Town ↝ Cidade
- ℵ   Tree ↝ Árvore
- ℵ   Trunk (of a Tree) ↝ Tronco
- ℵ   Wave ↝ Onda
- ℵ   Wind ↝ Vento

P.O.I. – Places of Interest

- ℵ   Beacon ↝ Faról
- ℵ   Cinema ↝ Cinema
- ℵ   Embassy ↝ Embaixada

א   Fire Station ↶ Estação de bombeiros

א   Hospital ↶ Hospital

א   Hotel ↶ Hotel

א   Museum ↶ Museu

א   Palace ↶ Palácio

א   Park ↶ Parque

א   Planetarium↶ Planetário

א   Police Station ↶ Estação da Polícia

א   Swimming Pool ↶ Piscina

א   Theater ↶ Teatro

א   Ticket Office ↶ Bilheteira

Religion

א   Agnostic ↶ Agnóstico

א   Atheist ↶ Ateu/ateia

א   Buddhist ↶ Budista

א   Catholic ↶ Católico

א   Christian ↶ Cristão

א   Church ↶ Igreja

א   God ↶ Deus

א   Jewish ↶ Judeu

א   Mosque ↶ Mesquita

א   Protestant ↶ Protestante

א   Religion ↶ Religião

א   Synagogue ↶ Sinagoga

א   Temple ↶ Templo

Abstract Nouns and Others

א   Actor ↶ Actor

א   Attic ↶ Sótão

א   Balance ↶ Saldo

- א Century ↪ Século
- א Cheap ↪ Barato
- א Class[64] ↪ Turma
- א Country ↪ País
- א Cry ↪ Choro
- א Degrees ↪ Graus
- א Distress ↪ Aflição
- א Earth ↪ Terra
- א Emergency ↪ Emergência
- א Emperor ↪ Imperador
- א European ↪ Europeu
- א Expensive ↪ Caro
- א Fleet ↪ Frota
- א Forecast ↪ Previsão
- א Generosity ↪ Generosidade
- א Happiness ↪ Felicidade
- א Help ↪ Ajuda/Socorro
- א High ↪ Alto/Alta
- א Journalist ↪ Jornalista
- א Joy ↪ Alegria
- א Judge ↪ Juiz
- א Jupiter ↪ Júpiter
- א Kindness ↪ Bondade
- א Knife ↪ Faca
- א Lost ↪ Perdido/Perdida
- א Low ↪ Baixo/Baixa
- א Manager ↪ Gestor/Gestora
- א Mars ↪ Marte
- א Mercury ↪ Mercúrio

---

64 If describing someone elegant, then use the word "classe."

ℵ Milky way ↝ Via láctea

ℵ Missing someone ↝ Saudade[65]

ℵ Neptune ↝ Neptuno

ℵ Opinion ↝ Opinião

ℵ Planet ↝ Planeta

ℵ Plate ↝ Prato

ℵ Pluto ↝ Plutão

ℵ Prescription ↝ Prescrição

ℵ Reader ↝ Leitor

ℵ Safety pin ↝ Pin de segurança

ℵ Salesman, seller, vendor ↝ Vendedor

ℵ Saturn ↝ Saturno

ℵ Scribe ↝ Escrivão

ℵ Sight ↝ Visão

ℵ Song ↝ Canção

ℵ State ↝ Estado

ℵ Student ↝ Aluno/estudante

ℵ Thought ↝ Pensamento

ℵ Uranus ↝ Urano

ℵ Urgent ↝ Urgente

ℵ Venus ↝ Vénus

ℵ View ↝ Vista

ℵ Writer ↝ Escritor

---

65 This is probably the most special word in Portuguese. It does not have a correspondent translation in any language. It describes us and is always present in the music that lives in our soul—Fado (Fate). Check out the diva, Amália Rodrigues, if you want to know more about "Fado" and "saudade."

Glossary of Verbs

You may have noticed that the previous list did not include any verbs. This is because the nouns and verbs have been separated to facilitate the search. Below, you will find a list of verbs that were **not** mentioned in the verbs chapter of the book.

א   Acabar ↰ (to) Finish

א   Acampar ↰ (to) Camp

א   Aceitar ↰ (to) Accept

א   Achar ↰ (to) Find

א   Acordar ↰ (to) Wake up

א   Adorar ↰ (to) Love, adore

א   Agir ↰ (to) Act

א   Ajudar ↰ (to) Help

א   Almoçar ↰ (to) Have lunch

א   Alugar ↰ (to) Rent

א   Andar ↰ (to) Walk

א   Apagar ↰ (to) Turn off, delete, erase

א   Aprender ↰ (to) Learn

א   Arrumar ↰ (to) Tidy up

א   Atravessar ↰ (to) Cross

א   Beber ↷ (to) Drink

א   Bocejar ↷ (to) Yawn

א   Brincar ↷ (to) Play (with something or someone)[66]

א   Cair ↷ (to) Fall

א   Caminhar ↷ (to) Walk

א   Cancelar ↷ (to) Cancel

א   Casar ↷ (to) Marry

א   Chamar ↷ (to) Call

א   Chegar ↷ (to) Arrive

א   Colocar ↷ (to) Put

א   Combinar ↷ (to) Arrange (a meeting, for example)

א   Começar ↷ (to) Start

א   Comprar ↷ (to) Buy

א   Continuar ↷ (to) Continue

א   Conversar ↷ (to) Talk

א   Convidar ↷ (to) Invite

א   Corrigir ↷ (to) Correct

א   Coser ↷ (to) Sew

א   Costumar ↷ Doing something very usually

א   Cozer ↷ (to) Boil

א   Cozinhar ↷ (to) Cook

א   Dançar ↷ (to) Dance

א   Deixar ↷ (to) Let go, or to leave alone

א   Descansar ↷ (to) Rest

א   Desejar ↷ (to) Wish

א   Desenhar ↷ (to) Draw

---

[66] It should be used in the following situations:

"I'm playing with my dog. ↷ Eu estou a brincar com o meu cão."

"The children are playing. ↷ As crianças estão a brincar."

"Go play with your toys. ↷ Vai brincar com os teus brinquedos."

א   Desligar ↶ (to) Turn off

א   Encontrar ↶ (to) Find

א   Entrar ↶ (to) Go in

א   Entregar ↶ (to) Deliver

א   Enviar ↶ (to) Send

א   Esperar ↶ (to) Wait

א   Explicar ↶ (to) Explain

א   Fechar ↶ (to) Close

א   Ficar ↶ (to) Stay

א   Florescer ↶ (to) Flourish

א   Gostar ↶ (to) Like

א   Guardar ↶ (to) Keep

א   Jantar ↶ (to) Have dinner

א   Jogar ↶ (to) Play

א   Lavar ↶ (to) Wash

א   Levantar ↶ (to) Lift

א   Levar ↶ (to) Take

א   Ligar ↶ (to) Connect

א   Limpar ↶ (to) Clean

א   Morar ↶ (to) Reside

א   Mudar ↶ (to) Change

א   Nadar ↶ (to) Swim

א   Necessitar ↶ (to) Need

א   Pagar ↶ (to) Pay

א   Parar ↶ (to) Stop

א   Passar ↶ (to) Pass

א   Pensar ↶ (to) Think

א   Perguntar ↶ (to) Ask

א   Pintar ↶ (to) Paint

א   Praticar ↶ (to) Practice

א   Precisar ↶ (to) Need

א   Pular ∽ (to) Jump, skip

א   Reservar ∽ (to) Book something (or to schedule a dinner reservation, for example)

א   Rir ∽ (to) Laugh

א   Sair ∽ (to) Leave, get out

א   Sentar ∽ (to) Sit

א   Soletrar ∽ (to) Spell

א   Sorrir ∽ (to) Smile

א   Telefonar ∽ (to) Phone/call someone

א   Tentar ∽ (to) Try

א   Terminar ∽ (to) Finish

א   Tocar ∽ (to) Touch, play

א   Tomar ∽ (to) Take

א   Trabalhar ∽ (to) Work

א   Trocar ∽ (to) Switch

א   Usar ∽ (to) Use, wear

א   Vender ∽ (to) Sell

א   Viajar ∽ (to) Travel

א   Virar ∽ (to) Turn

א   Visitar ∽ (to) Visit

א   Voar ∽ (to) Fly

א   Voltar ∽ (to) Return

Common mistakes

Portuguese is indeed a tricky language, even for natives. Thus, there a few mistakes that everyone makes at some point, especially beginners, when speaking or writing in Portuguese. To help you identify those mistakes easily—and to try and avoid them in the future—here are of the most commonly made mistakes by beginners in the Portuguese language.

To start, let's go through the rules of capitalization[67]. This mistake happens quite often with fluent speakers, or rather, writers.

<u>Uppercase</u> should be used in the following cases:

ℵ   Beginning of any sentence (e.g., <u>A</u> bola é minha.);

ℵ   Proper nouns (e.g., <u>C</u>arlos);

ℵ   Names of fictitious characters or cognomens (mainly applied to kings, e.g., D. Dinis, o *Lavrador* ⌣ D. Dinis, the *Farmer*)[68];

---

67 Keep in mind that this guide is **not** using the Orthographic Agreement of 1990. You probably will see this rule applied differently, depending on whether the author writes under the agreement.

68 The "*D.*" stands for "*Dom*," which is an honorific title prefixed to the names of royal family members. It means "*master*" in Latin.

א   Names of populations, races, tribes, castes, religious entities, and their beliefs (e.g., **D**eus ↩ God; Os **P**ortugueses são animados. ↩ The Portuguese are cheerful.);

א   Mythological and astronomical names (e.g., **Z**eus ↩ Zeus);

א   Geographical names (toponyms), streets, rivers, mountains (e.g., **P**ortugal, **L**isboa, rio **D**ouro, serra da **E**strela);

א   Months (e.g., **D**ezembro ↩ December);

א   Seasons of the year (e.g., **P**rimavera ↩ Spring);

א   Holidays and festive activities (e.g., **N**atal ↩ Christmas);

א   Cardinal points (e.g., **S**udoeste ↩ Southwest);

א   Abbreviations of the cardinal points (e.g., **NO** ↩ NW);

א   Names of institutions, institutes, organizations, associations, etc. (e.g., **E**scola **S**ecundária de Santo André ↩ Santo André High School);

א   Book titles and publications (e.g., **O**s **L**usíadas[69]);

א   Honorific titles and pronouns referring to a god (e.g., **M**ajestade ↩ Majesty, **E**le (Deus) ↩ He (God));

א   Historical facts (e.g., **R**evolução Francesa ↩ French Revolution);

א   Official acts (e.g., **D**ecreto-lei ↩ Decree-law);

א   Acronyms (e.g., **EUA** ↩ USA).

Lowercase should be used in the following cases:

א   Common use of everyday vocabulary;

א   Days of the week (e.g., Hoje é **s**egunda-feira.);

א   Names of populations when used as adjectives (e.g., A comida **p**ortuguesa é boa. ↩ The Portuguese food is good.);

---

69 The most famous Portuguese epic poem by Luís de Camões.

ℵ Geographical terms, such as river or mountain, are used before the names (e.g., <u>r</u>io Mondego, <u>s</u>erra de Monchique).

Now, let's see a few more common mistakes that natives make all the time. These mistakes are learned, so beginners probably won't pick up the bad habits, provided, of course, that they identify these mistakes when they see them being used by natives:

ℵ **A gente *vai*, ou *vamos*?**

In English, it would be something like "the people go, or goes?" The problem is how the verb is conjugated. Even though "gente" refers to a group of people, it is in its singular form, hence the verb being conjugated accordingly in the third-person singular. If it were "As gentes," then the verb would be conjugated in the third-person plural, "As gentes *vão*." If we said instead, "nós," then the verb would be conjugated in the first-person plural, "Nós *vamos*."

ℵ **Á? Nope**

There is no such word. "À," on the other hand, exists—it derives from the contraction between the preposition "a," and the defined article "a." Example: "Eu vou <u>à</u> escola. – I'm going to school." The accent mark is acute.

ℵ **Bad ≠ badly**

The first translates to "mau," while the second translates to "mal." The first one is always an adjective; the second is an adverb or a noun. In Brazilian Portuguese, the accent will make the two words sound very similar.

"O Voldermort é **mau** – Voldemort is bad."

"MAL" as an adverb: "Isto está **mal** feito – This is done badly."

Or

"MAL" as a noun: "O bem luta contra o **mal** – The good fights evil."

ℵ How many years ago?

It is very common to see, even from good writers, sentences like "Há três anos atrás - Three years ago." The problem is that the sentence in Portuguese is a bit redundant, just like if we added "back" to the sentence in English (Yes, it does not make sense, but it is just to make it easier to understand the problem). So, "Three years ago back" is needless. The same goes for the Portuguese sentence. You can either say "Há três anos" or "Três anos atrás," both meaning "Three years ago."

ℵ Isn't it going up the hill a bit redundant?

The translation in Portuguese sure is. "Going up" is "subir" in Portuguese, and "cima" means "up." So, in Portuguese, "subir para cima" is describing a reality in which the verb "subir" already does by itself. Because you cannot really "subir para baixo" or "going up down the hill"...

Mas ≠ mais

This is another example of how the Brazilian Portuguese accent might affect the understanding of some words and create a few mistakes. In Brazilian Portuguese, they are pronounced very similarly. "Mas" is a conjunction that indicates contrast. It translates to "but." On the other hand, "mais" is an adverb related to the quantity of things. It translates to "more."

Example: "**Mas** eu não ir! - But I don't want to go!"

"Eu quero **mais** chocolate. - I want more chocolate."

ℵ Now that we know there's no á, what about "há"?

"Há" is from the transitive verb "haver" that can have different translations in English, depending on its use. However, remember to know when to use "h" so that you can substitute it in your head by the verb "existir - exist," and it would still make sense, even though it won't sound that great. So:

e.g.: "**Há** banana? - Is there banana?"

Or

"**Existe** banana? – Does banana exist?"

See that if we said, "Vou **à** escola – I'm going to school," we couldn't change it to "Vou **existe** escola – I'm going exists school." It just wouldn't make any sense. Basically, the "há" indicates that there is something, that something exists, that someone has it. If that is not what you want to indicate, then you should use the "à." Notice that it has an acute accent mark, instead of a grave one, when it's by itself.

Bear in mind that when it comes to describing how time passes—how many years or hours have passed—like it was mentioned above, "há" doesn't have the meaning of "exist" or "there is."

ℵ Obrigado/a

This is a very common mistake and one that is very understandably made by foreigners. This might be because of how it is perpetuated by the natives that say both "Obrigado" or "Obrigada" indistinctively. It's not that they know, but the fluency and speed of speaking the language end up confusing anyone who is not used to hearing a language that sometimes varies in gender (and number, as we know). However, this word, which means "thank you," must agree with the gender of the speaker and *NOT* with the gender of whoever you are speaking with. So, if you are a man, you should always say, "Obrigad**o**." If you are a woman, you should always say, "Obrigad**a**."

ℵ ProntO *not* prontoS

There is no significant explanation for how this word was born. "Pronto" means "ready," as in "Isto está **pronto** – This is ready." However, it can also be used as a crutch or an interjection, just like "enough!" or "that's that!" With no "s" at the end, *pronto*!

ℵ Quaisquer*es*?

"Qualquer" and "quaisquer." Singular and plural, respectively. "Quaisqueres" does not exist. The plural is done with the part "qual/quais" and not "quer/queres."

Example: "Eu quero uma bola qualquer. - I want any/whatever ball."

"Eu quero umas bolas quaisquer. - I want any/whatevers balls."

ℵ "S" or no "s"?

You should have noticed that if you use a verb conjugated in the second-person plural, you often have to add an "s" at the end of the word. If you are, instead, conjugating it in the second-person singular, there is no "s," even though many people misuse it when speaking.

Example: "Tu fizeste**s** a cama?" is wrong. It should be: "Tu **fizeste** a cama? - Did you make your bed?"

"Ontem foste**s** à praia?" is wrong. It should be: "Ontem **foste** à praia. - Yesterday you went to the beach."

ℵ The correct way to write it is "com certeza" - com certeza!

Even though it sounds very much the same, "concerteza" and "com certeza" are spelled differently. One is also plain wrong. "Com certeza" means "surely" or "for sure" and "with certainty" literally.

ℵ There were many... ↶ Haviam muitas... ou havia muitas...?

The verb "haver" has no plural form whenever we are referring to a quantity of things, using it in the way that it translates to the verb "to exist" and not referring to the verb "to have"—the verb simply does not adapt. It is always used in the singular form, even when conjugated in different tenses.

Example: In the present tense

"**Há** uma pêra aqui. - There is one pear here."

"**Há** muitas uvas aqui. - There are a lot of grapes here."

In the past imperfect

"**Havia** um café na esquina. - There was one cafe shop at the corner."

"**Havia** dois cinemas na cidade. – There were two cinemas in town."

Who (or What) Can You Trust?

**Some words seem to exist to mess with us... Why would two words that are spelled almost exactly the same mean something different? Basically, there are several words, which are called the false cognates—also known as false friends—that may look and/or sound the same in English and Portuguese but have completely different meanings. Hence the *false* in "false friends"—it looks like they might help you but trusting them would just end up in betrayal. The tricky thing about them is that you do not know who those friends are until you know who they really are. And by then, it may be too late—as you have made a fool out of yourself! In conclusion, it is better to be safe than sorry[70] because there is no way of knowing them by following a rule. What you have to do instead is try to memorize them. To get there, you always have to double-check the meaning of a word that seems familiar, and most of all, pay attention to the context. Not everything is bad, though—there are also true long-lasting friendships. Some similar words in both languages are translated with the same meaning, sometimes only by slightly changing the suffix. The following are examples of both groups.

---

70 Or as we say in Portuguese, "É melhor prevenir do que remediar!"

Trust me not

ENGLISH WORD	PORTUGUESE TRANSLATION	FALSE FRIEND	TRANSLATION
Actually	Na verdade, realmente	Actualmente	Nowadays, currently
Beef	Vaca	Bife	Steak
Data	Dados, informação	Data	Date (of a calendar)
Exit	Saída	Êxito	Success
Expert	Especialista, perito	Esperto	Smart, savvy
Exquisite	Magnífico, requintado	Esquisito	Strange, weird
Lunch	Almoço	Lanche	Snack (usually, in the afternoon)
Parents	Pais (Mãe e Pai)	Parentes	Relatives
Policy	Políticas, regulamento,	Polícia	Police

Trust me![71]

As mentioned, some words you can rely on. Let's check out some examples and the set of rules you have to follow to impress your friends, family, and colleagues. If you end up relying on a false friend and making a mistake, that is ok—they probably won't even notice.

So, for words ending in:

⤳   ly - switch it for **mente**;

⤳   ence - switch it for **ência**;

⤳

---

71 Even though this happens quite often, there are also many cases in which the rule is not followed, and the translation occurs through a different process. Always double-check!

ty - switch it for **dade**;

→ **tion** - switch it for **ção.**

LY / MENTE:

Brutally = Bruta + lly ↶ Brutal - ly + mente = Brutalmente

Casually ↶ Casual**mente**

Cruelly ↶ Cruel**mente**

Eventually ↶ Eventual**mente**

Fatally ↶ Fatal**mente**

Globally ↶ Global**mente**

Ideally ↶ Ideal**mente**

Nasally ↶ Nasal**mente**

Totally ↶ Total**mente**

Verbally ↶ Verbal**mente**

ENCE / ÊNCIA

Competence = Compet + ence ↶ Compet - ence + ência = Competência

Consequence ↶ Consequ**ência**

Consistence ↶ Consist**ência**

Convalescence ↶ Convalesc**ência**

Correspondence ↶ Correspond**ência**

Experience ↶ Experi**ência**

Inconvenience ↶ Inconveni**ência**

Independence ↶ Independ**ência**

Influence ↶ Influ**ência**

Negligence ↶ Neglig**ência**

TY / DADE:

Ability = Abili + ty ↝ Abili – ty + dade = Habilidade

Agility ↝ Agilidade

Clarity ↝ Claridade

Gravity ↝ Gravidade

Incompatibility ↝ Incompatibilidade

Obesity ↝ Obesidade

Parity ↝ Paridade

Reality ↝ Realidade

Sexuality ↝ Sexualidade

Utility ↝ Utilidade

TION / ÇÃO:

Action = Ac + tion ↝ Ac - tion + ção = Acção

Attention ↝ Atenção

Education ↝ Educação

Lotion ↝ Loção

Nation ↝ Nação

Notion ↝ Noção

Option ↝ Opção

Potion ↝ Poção

Situation ↝ Situação

Solution ↝ Solução

Finally, we have the blessed cognates. These are words that, in contrast to the "trust me not's," are similar or the same in English and Portuguese while keeping the same meaning. Check out the list to get to know a few examples—but **ALWAYS DOUBLE-CHECK!**

ℵ   Acidental ↬ Accidental

ℵ   Ácido ↫ Acid

ℵ   Adversário ↫ Adversary

ℵ   Adversidade ↬ Adversity

ℵ   Agência ↬ Agency

ℵ   Agente ↫ Agent

ℵ   Alarmante ↬ Alarming

ℵ   Alarme ↬ Alarm

ℵ   Ar ↫ Air

ℵ   Área ↫ Area

ℵ   Arte ↫ Art

ℵ   Artista ↫ Artist

ℵ   Actividade ↬ Activity

ℵ   Activista ↫ Activist

ℵ   Atmosfera ↬ Atmosphere

ℵ   Aventura ↫ Adventure

ℵ   Cafeteria ↫ Cafeteria

ℵ   Calculadora ↬ Calculator

ℵ   Calcular ↫ Calculate

ℵ   Câmara ↫ Camera

ℵ   Centro ↫ Center

ℵ   Cinema ↫ Cinema

ℵ   Classe ↫ Class

ℵ   Comédia ↫ Comedy

ℵ   Companhia ↬ Company

ℵ   Computador ↬ Computer

ℵ   Construção ↫ Construction

ℵ   Construir ↫ Construct

ℵ   Continental ↫ Continental

ℵ   Continente ↫ Continent

ℵ   Controlo ↫ Control

א   Debate ↻ Debate

א   Desastre ↻ Disaster

א   Diferente ↻ Different

א   Direcção ↻ Direction

א   Direcções ↻ Directions

א   Director ↻ Director

א   Distância ↻ Distance

א   Distante ↻ Distant

א   Editar ↻ Edit

א   Elevador ↻ Elevator

א   Elevar ↻ Elevate

א   Emoção ↻ Emotion

א   Errático ↻ Erratic

א   Erro ↻ Error

א   Exame ↻ Exam

א   Exacto ↻ Exact

א   Exemplo ↻ Example

א   Explodir ↻ Explode

א   Explosão ↻ Explosion

א   Facto ↻ Fact

א   Factor ↻ Factor

א   Familiar ↻ Familiar

א   Festival ↻ Festival

א   Fotocópia ↻ Photocopy

א   Frequente ↻ Frequent

א   Funeral ↻ Funeral

א   Futuro ↻ Future

א   Galáctico ↻ Galactic

א   Galáxia ↻ Galaxy

א   Grupo ↻ Group

א   Hipnose ↻ Hypnosis

א   Humanitário ↶ Humanitarian

א   Humano ↶ Human

א   Humanóide ↶ Humanoid

א   Ideal ↶ Ideal

א   Ideia ↶ Idea

א   Idêntico ↶ Identical

א   Identidade ↶ Identity

א   Identificação ↶ Identification

א   Independência ↶ Independence

א   Independente ↶ Independent

א   Infernal ↶ Infernal

א   Informação ↶ Information

א   Insecticida ↶ Insecticide

א   Inspecção ↶ Inspection

א   Inspector ↶ Inspector

א   Inteligência ↶ Intelligence

א   Inteligente ↶ Intelligent

א   Lista ↶ List

א   Literatura ↶ Literature

א   Magia ↶ Magic

א   Maneira ↶ Manner

א   Mapa ↶ Map

א   Massagem ↶ Massage

א   Matemática ↶ Mathematics

א   Memória ↶ Memory

א   Mensagem ↶ Message

א   Metal ↶ Metal

א   Metálico ↶ Metallic

א   Microfone ↶ Microphone

א   Minuto ↶ Minute

א   Momento ↶ Moment

ℵ   Música ↩ Music

ℵ   Objectivo ↩ Objective

ℵ   Objecto ↩ Object

ℵ   Observatório ↩ Observatory

ℵ   Ocasião ↩ Occasion

ℵ   Oceano ↩ Ocean

ℵ   Ordinário[72] ↩ Ordinary

ℵ   Paciência ↩ Patience

ℵ   Paciente ↩ Patient

ℵ   Pânico ↩ Panic

ℵ   Parcial ↩ Partial

ℵ   Parte ↩ Part

ℵ   Perfume ↩ Perfume

ℵ   Perímetro ↩ Perimeter

ℵ   Planeta ↩ Planet

ℵ   Presente ↩Present

ℵ   Privado ↩ Private

ℵ   Problema ↩ Problem

ℵ   Problemático ↩ Problematic

ℵ   Rádio ↩ Radio

ℵ   Radioactivo ↩ Radioactive

ℵ   Restaurante ↩ Restaurant

ℵ   Série ↩ Series

ℵ   Sério ↩ Serious

ℵ   Teste ↩ Test

ℵ   Texto ↩ Text

ℵ   Turista ↩ Tourist

ℵ   Uniforme ↩ Uniform

---

72 Besides normal or common, "Ordinário" may also mean vulgar, indecent, trashy. It will depend on the context, so if you are flirting with someone and they call you "ordinário/a," it was probably not a successful attempt at romance!

א   Universal ↪ Universal

א   Universo ↪ Universe

א   Usual ↪ Usual

א   Vénus ↪Venus

א   Virgem ↪ Virgin

א   Zona ↪ Zone

Do You Speak Brazilian?

Portuguese is becoming a high-demand language, and that is due mainly to Brazil's rising popularity and the role it plays in the world's economy. This book, however, was written following Portuguese from Portugal "rules," which differ slightly from the Portuguese from Brazil. Nevertheless, it might be confusing for beginners to understand one type if they are used to hearing or studying the other. So, now that you have almost mastered this beautiful language, check this small list, with a few selected examples, which present some common words that change whether you are speaking Portuguese from Portugal or Portuguese from Brazil.

ENGLISH	PORTUGUESE FROM PORTUGAL	PORTUGUESE FROM BRAZIL
Bathroom	Casa de banho	Banheiro
Breakfast	Pequeno-almoço	Café da manhã
Bus	Autocarro	Ônibus
Cell phone	Telemóvel	Celular
City Hall	Câmara municipal	Prefeitura
Fridge	Frigorífico	Geladeira
Grass	Relva	Gramado
Ice cream	Gelado	Sorvete
Juice	Sumo	Suco
Nap	Sesta	Cochilo
Persimmon	Dióspiro	Caqui
Police station	Esquadra da polícia	Delegacia
Suit	Fato	Terno
Toilet seat	Sanita	Vaso
Truck	Camião	Caminhão
Weight room	Ginásio	Academia

O FIM[73] – CONCLUSION

Congratulations on making it through to the end of this book! Learning a language is never easy—and Portuguese is **no** exception.

Now, you have learned the basics of the Portuguese language. Even though you are at a beginner's level (or a bit beyond it), this guide should have provided a solid foundation or an excellent reinforcement to Portuguese.

The book aimed for an upbeat and dynamic rhythm that would make it easy to follow. To aid the creation of an exciting environment for learning, it built the chapters via a light or informal writing style, throwing in, at times, a bit of humor!

Aside from all the learning, it should have been a fun ride and spiked your interest in the language, motivating you to continue studying it.

To conclude, please come back to this guide whenever needed. The valuable content will hopefully help you create memories of a fun journey to another country and culture, which will allow you to get closer to other people. It should remind you of the best there is in life—connecting.

---

73 The recommended song for this chapter is "O Fim" by B-Fachada.

Printed in the USA
CPSIA information can be obtained
at www.ICGtesting.com
LVHW012319081223
765728LV00006B/197